Has He Made
A Difference

Black Victory

Black Victory

□CARL STOKES
and the WINNING
OF CLEVELAND
by Kenneth G. Weinberg

Chicago / Quadrangle Books / 1968

*To all those political experts who were
convinced that a Negro could not be elected
mayor of a city where white voters outnumber
Negroes by almost two to one*

Preface

THERE are black people in this country who claim they want to burn our cities down. There are other blacks, hopefully more numerous, who want to build our cities up. Carl B. Stokes, mayor of Cleveland, is a builder and not a burner, but it would take a miracle worker to cure the urban disease that infects Cleveland, Ohio, perhaps more critically than any other urban area in the United States. It is unreasonable to expect that the deterioration of our cities that has occurred under the rule of white mayors can, in the foreseeable future, be cured by black mayors.

The significance of the election of a Carl Stokes lies elsewhere. He has, for the time being at least, demonstrated that black political activity can provide a viable alternative to violence in our cities, and that demonstration may buy the time needed for the country to find the will and the means to attack the crisis of the cities and to heal the awful breach between the races that seems, in this spring of 1968, to be growing ever wider. "The Fire Next Time" has become a prophecy fulfilled, and the mind reels under shrill cries of separatism, nationalism, Malcolm Xism, and a sad prediction by the President of the United States that our cities will almost surely experience several more summers of violence.

Carl Stokes has already bought valuable time for Cleveland. If nothing else happens in his entire administration, it must still be reckoned a success because Cleveland, almost alone among the big cities with histories of racial disorders, experienced no violence or unrest in the wake of the assassination of Stokes's mentor and friend, Martin Luther King. In the days following that terrible event, while New York, Chicago, Baltimore, Detroit, Pittsburgh, Washington, and other cities suffered another round of burning and looting, Cleveland remained calm. This was not because the city's ghetto Negroes were indifferent to King's martyrdom. King had spent several weeks in Cleveland during the 1967 mayoralty campaign, and the black people of Cleveland knew and loved King well and were as furious at his murder as the rest of the country. But black Cleveland also loves Carl Stokes, and during those first fearful nights they listened to their mayor, who walked among them all night, every night, alone and unguarded, urging patience and understanding and reason.

The absence of a Martin Luther King makes the presence of a Carl Stokes all the more important. There are too few moderate voices left and there is too little time remaining.

The President's Commission on Civil Disorders has had no discernible effect, despite its bold and courageous report, warning us once again that America is running out of time. The report has been applauded by most well-meaning people and institutions; it has even proved to be a best-seller in paperback reprint—showing no more, perhaps, than that what Americans like to read about when they can't read about sex is violence.

This book is about neither. It is about the election of a Negro mayor in a city with a white majority of almost two to one—an event that may cast a slight ray of light in the dark horizon stretching over all those endless summers. The commission's report seems doomed to be filed and forgotten. Congress is apparently impotent to act on it, and the President, as he has done on other issues, seems to have taken it as a personal affront. Indeed, he acts as though he wishes it hadn't happened.

But Carl Stokes has happened and he will continue to happen—on the national as well as the local scene. History may judge him a good, bad, or indifferent mayor, but he has earned his place in history by insisting on his

right to govern a city, be it wisely or unwisely, coura-
geously or timidly, firmly or passively, as well as or as
poorly as any white man.

I have known Carl Stokes for many years, and think
him a remarkable man doing as fine a job as can be expected at a time when complete success must depend on
a national commitment to a solution of the urban crisis.
And I think his story important because the Cleveland
experience is certain to be repeated soon in Chicago,
Detroit, Newark, Los Angeles, New York, and other urban areas with large Negro populations, and Cleveland
politics is like politics anywhere, only more so.

I am neither a biographer nor a political scientist, but
merely a fascinated, if sometimes horrified, observer of
the Cleveland political scene, and I have attempted to
set down here only my personal observations of that
scene and the man who now dominates it.

So far as I know, I have neither altered nor invented
any facts; however, the inferences and conclusions drawn
from those facts may be arguable. To that extent, I do
not claim to be telling it like it is, but only like it seems
to me.

Contents

Black Victory

Introduction

ON NOVEMBER 7, 1967, in Cleveland, Ohio, Carl Burton Stokes, a forty-year-old Democrat, became the first Negro to have been elected mayor of a major American city. Stokes received 129,829 votes as against 127,328 for Seth Taft, his Republican opponent.

In heavily Democratic Cleveland, the crucial contest had occurred a month earlier on October 3, when Stokes won the Democratic primary over party-endorsed Ralph Locher, the third-term incumbent mayor. The margin of victory approximated the number of votes cast for Stokes in white wards—18,000.

It is, of course, no great feat for a Democrat to be elected mayor of Cleveland, a nationality oriented city with strong labor-union influence, where the Democratic voter registration exceeds the Republican by more than five to one. Democrats Frank Lausche, Thomas Burke, Anthony Celebrezze, and Ralph Locher, each with his own special appeal to one or more of Cleveland's various nationality groups, had enjoyed an unbroken line of succession to city hall since 1941. But Carl Stokes is a Democrat of a different color.

How did it happen that a city which in recent years had suffered from a notoriously poor record in race relations would suddenly appear to lead the nation in political maturity? Cleveland's smug slogan, "The Best Location in the Nation," was spoken only in mockery and embarrassment in the middle 1960's, years that produced a devastating riot in Hough, one of the nation's worst slum areas (and Cleveland has others to match it), and a vicious racial incident in Murray Hill, the so-called Little Italy section of Cleveland; years that saw Cleveland sink into a numbing stupor of despair and frustration with pollution of the spirit threatening to match that of its air and waterways.

What forces, then, and what manner of man enabled Cleveland voters to elect the black son of a laundry-worker father and a domestic-servant mother over Seth Taft, the grandson of a President, son of a mayor, nephew of a senator, and cousin of a congressman?

1. THE DROP-OUT

SETH TAFT can trace his American heritage back to the early 1600's when both his paternal and maternal ancestors emigrated to Massachusetts from England. Carl Stokes's American lineage may very well extend back as far, but, except for the last century, the Stokeses have been invisible to history.

We do know that in 1909, when Seth's grandfather, William Howard Taft, the twenty-seventh President of the United States, was moving his three-hundred-pound girth and his oversize bathtub into the White House,

Carl Stokes's grandfather was trying to scratch out a meager living on a tenant farm far below the Mason-Dixon line.

Grandfather Taft, of course, became Chief Justice of the United States Supreme Court after leaving the White House, and his son Charles, Seth's father, became mayor of Cincinnati. His other son, Robert, became Mr. Republican as a United States senator from Ohio, and *his* son, Robert, is now Cincinnati's member in the United States House of Representatives.

Carl Stokes's grandfather continued to be a tenant farmer and part-time preacher for the rest of his life, while *his* son, Carl's father, spent most of his short life —thirty-nine years—as an unskilled laborer in a laundry in Cleveland.

If anyone was destined for a political career, it was Seth Taft. If anyone wasn't, it was Carl Stokes.

Seth Taft would begin fulfilling that destiny as soon as he was out of knee pants. Following a path well laid out by many Tafts before him, he would attend an eastern prep school, then Yale University, and finally Yale Law School. The Robert Taft branch of the family had, by the mid-forties, staked out Cincinnati as a private political preserve, and to avoid competition with cousin Robert, Seth moved north to join the prestigious Cleveland law firm of Jones, Day, Cockley, and Reavis, which, with its sixty-five lawyers, was virtually a political power base in itself.

Carl Stokes had no such path to follow. With the death of his father in 1930, it was a question not of which school to attend but of how to survive. To be widowed, unemployed, and penniless is hardly a happy state of affairs at any time, but in the 1930's it was catastrophic. Nevertheless, Louise Stokes was determined to keep her family together, and, after a short period on relief, was able to support herself and her two young sons (Carl, two; Louis, four) on the slight wages she earned as a domestic servant. Both boys did well in school in the east side Negro neighborhood in which they lived, and as soon as they could they supplemented the family income by selling newspapers and running errands.

Carl Stokes was street-wise before he was ten. Before he was sixteen, he was a high school drop-out. Most of Cleveland's East Tech Negro graduates were going straight into factory work, now that defense production had eased the unemployment problem. Why bother with a high school diploma when you could get that same job without one? Besides, his family could use the extra money, and so the year 1944 found seventeen-year-old Carl Stokes inspecting valves for the Thompson Products Company during the day and practicing boxing at night.

Carl's first boxing lessons had been on the streets, and since he won more often than he lost, his ambition for a time zeroed in on a boxing career. Thompson Products held no future for him. After all, when you've inspected one valve, you've inspected them all. Prize fighting, in the 1940's, offered one of the few avenues of escape for a Negro youth from a life in the laundry, the elevator, the shoe-shine stand, or the factory.

Jackie Robinson had not yet broken the color line in

baseball, and pro football was almost as lily white; but Joe Louis, Sugar Ray Robinson, and Henry Armstrong had made it big in boxing. If Carl could only sharpen up that left hook, maybe he could, too.

Stokes graduated from Golden Gloves competition to club fights for $50 purses (from which he carries two scars on his forehead), and in between bouts he found time to become one of the best pool players in the neighborhood. At the same time, having always been encouraged by his mother to read as much as possible, he continued to bring home library books, even though, as he has said, "reading was against the mores of the neighborhood," and the books had to be smuggled home under his coat. And so it went—boxing, pool, books—until one day in 1945, when Uncle Sam wanted *him*.

Carl's tour of duty with the army of occupation in Germany in 1945 and 1946 did little for his boxing style but much for his perspective. The world did indeed consist of more than east-side pool halls and gymnasiums. And it was full of people—most of them white, at least in that part of the world, and when he began to measure himself against this white world—corporals and sergeants, lieutenants and captains, who were also teachers, lawyers, engineers, doctors, businessmen—it seemed to him that he could think as well as they, talk as well, see things just as clearly. He lacked only two things that they had—a white skin and an education. Their skin they could have, but he would have their education. Thus, upon his discharge from the army, he immediately re-entered East Tech High School, graduated in 1947 at the age of twenty, and prepared to enter college.

That same year Seth Taft, fresh from Yale Law School, was preparing to join Jones, Day, Cockley, and Reavis, and Ralph Locher, a thirty-two-year-old Cleveland lawyer, was about to become one of Governor Frank Lausche's assistants in Columbus. Both Locher and Taft must sometimes have ruefully wished that Carl Stokes had had a better left hook.

2. THE STUDENT

FOR THE next ten years Carl Stokes worked and studied his way through three colleges and law school. West Virginia State College for two years, night school at Cleveland College while working for the Ohio State Department of Liquor Control, and then a year at the University of Minnesota, where, to support himself, he worked as a dining-car waiter on the *Rock Island Rocket* between Minneapolis and Dallas—doing the first part of his homework in Minnesota before the first course, and finishing in Texas after the last.

Though Carl traveled far at Minnesota, his money did not, and he returned to Cleveland to finish law school at night at Cleveland Marshall while holding a job as a municipal-court probation officer during the day. Finally, in 1958, his law degree earned, he received an appointment to the law department of the city of Cleveland as an assistant police prosecutor. Liquor-department enforcement and municipal-court probation work, useful as these jobs were to Carl's education, are only the elevator operator and handyman jobs of political life. But now he was in the prosecutor's office, where the white folks worked. Carl B. Stokes was about to start his long climb to the executive suite.

The municipal criminal court is the side of the face of city government most often seen by the public, and in the case of the poor, especially the Negro poor, it is often the only side with which they have any contact. Unfortunately, it is also the side of the face with all the warts on it. All crimes classified as misdemeanors, including traffic offenses, come under the jurisdiction of that court, and the case load produced by a complex urban society cannot be handled by machinery and facilities that were inadequate even for a far more simple society years ago.

In 1921, alarmed by what appeared to be a breakdown of criminal justice in Cleveland, the Cleveland Foundation, a well-endowed charitable trust whose funds and whose policy, to a large extent, are controlled by the Cleveland Trust Company, underwrote the Cleveland Crime Survey, under the direction of Roscoe Pound and Felix Frankfurter, of the Harvard Law School. The survey culminated in a report—"Criminal Justice in Cleveland"—more than seven hundred pages long, most of them critical of the overcrowded, undermanned, mal-administered criminal court in which any idea of justice could only be a dim memory.

And yet, by 1958 no action had been taken by the city of Cleveland on any of the survey's recommendations, and conditions were, in fact, worse than they had been in 1921. This same paralysis had afflicted the other branches of city hall as well, more noticeably since 1941, when Frank Lausche became the first of Cleveland's care-taker mayors who took care of industry but not of the city's problems: the noxious fumes, smoke, and debris that were being spewed out into the air and waterways of Cleveland by the factories, for example; or public housing, which was, of course, a dirty word ("socialism") at city hall.

As downtown deteriorated, as slum areas festered with disease and resentment, as the citizens of Cleveland became more alienated from their government, the real power of the city—the great corporations, their great law firms, and their great banker, the Cleveland Trust Company (whose portfolios held large chunks of the corporations' stock, and on whose boards of directors sat Cleveland Trust officials)—cheered on by the newspapers, and especially by the *Cleveland Press,* elected and re-elected these honest, decent, attractive do-nothing mayors and what they did not do best was rock the boat.

For twenty-five years, all that had been required from city hall was honesty, humility, and a balanced budget.

Nothing must be done to interfere with industry's right to make as much money as possible, as fast as possible. The end of World War II found Cleveland with 100,000 new residents, mostly Negroes, who had migrated north to get rich in the defense plants. There was no housing to accommodate these newcomers, and the proud old homes on Euclid Avenue and in the Hough area soon became rooming-houses and apartments. Some remained single-family residences occupied by multiple families, friends, and relatives.

Cleveland had been very proud of itself in 1927 for adopting one of the country's first and most comprehensive zoning laws, which was to provide for the orderly and esthetic development of the city by restricting land use and creating separate zones for homes, apartments, and commercial and industrial buildings.

But zoning requirements were overlooked during the war, and by war's end it was already too late. Great sections of Cleveland's east side had already become a slum, and landlords were hot-footing it over to city council to obtain zoning ordinances and special permits for multiple occupancy of single-family dwellings. It was easier, of course, if one had a friend in council, and the increased profits to be gained from such arrangements, or from the privilege of a service station or warehouse or tavern in a residential area, more than justified the price of that friendship.

As the east-side slum spread outward, there was a mass exodus to the suburbs; but not all who could afford it could flee, since most of the suburbs, by one device or another, were determined to stay as white as they were.

The nationality groups on the east side—the middle, eastern, and southern European communities—generally held their ground, but began to feel encroached upon by the expanding Negro ghettos.

A far different pattern applied to that portion of the city lying to the west of the Cuyahoga River (possibly the most polluted stream in America). The west side had, in fact, at one time been a separate city, called Ohio City, and its composition was and still is strikingly different from that of the east side. Its people are mostly Irish, German, and Anglo-Saxon, and its neighborhoods have managed to avoid the decay of the east side.

By 1960 Cleveland had, in effect, become three separate communities—the white west side, the Negro east side, and the nationality groups south and southeast side, each constituting roughly a third of Cleveland's 900,000 population. It was almost entirely a working-class (when employed) population, much of the wealth and intellect of the city having fled to the suburbs.

What had happened to Cleveland had happened to almost all the large American cities, but Cleveland was the slowest in recognizing its urban crisis. It had carried the maxim of governing best by governing least to a ridiculous extreme. And what was apparent to the country as a whole before it became obvious to city hall now, sadly, appears to be plain to the whole world. Ian McDonald, writing in the London *Times,* on July 16, 1967, said:

Cleveland, the nation's eighth largest city, appears to an observer to be swiftly submerging under the accumulated weight of its many intractable problems. Even Clevelanders refer to it as a provincial place; and there is little of the community spirit among its wealthy families, who proved to be the salvation of Pittsburgh and Minneapolis.

Welcome to city hall, Carl B. Stokes.

3. THE PROSECUTOR

THE NEW assistant police prosecutor set out to join battle in the jungle that is Cleveland's municipal criminal court. Amid harassed and callous fellow prosecutors; amid cynical judges who had long since despaired of hoping to administer justice in the mass-production system of hearings made necessary by the case load; amid unsmiling, unhappy, overworked bureaucrats; amid telephone-booth lawyers who haunt the halls of criminal courts, Carl Stokes soon began to stand out. Fresh from law school with a zeal for seeing justice done, and his sensitivity not yet dulled by the deadening crush of a never-ending stream of society's losers, Carl approached his work with a degree of energy and enthusiasm not often seen in Cleveland municipal court, and it wasn't long before he became the man to see in the prosecutor's office. He was friendly, he was knowledgeable, he would listen, he was fair, he was forceful.

Stokes was both delighted and alarmed by what he learned in that first year. Delighted because he realized at the very outset that he was well equipped to handle the job, alarmed and appalled by the low state to which city government had sunk.

For four years Stokes had daily contact with a wide cross-section of Cleveland's people—affluent whites involved in traffic offenses, alcoholic whites from skid row, bewildered and helpless Negroes, ready to submit to any indignity the law wished to inflict on them, and defiant black nationalists contemptuous of Stokes as a representative of the Man's idea of justice.

And always there were the sullen, hostile, bitter faces of Negro youths waging their endless war on a society that had written them off—a society that offered them inferior and overcrowded schools, substandard housing, unemployment, contempt and abuse from the police, and the massive indifference of the white world that had always run Cleveland. Bad trouble was brewing, and Carl was determined to do something about it. But the prosecutor's office deals only with the results of trouble, not with the causes or the remedies. Those would have to be attacked by city hall.

City hall in Cleveland lies only fifteen short blocks from criminal court, but Carl decided to reach it via the state legislature in Columbus, Ohio, 150 miles away. In March 1962 he submitted his resignation to his boss, the man who had hired him, Ralph Locher, the law director of the city of Cleveland. When Frank Lausche had left the governor's mansion to go to the United States Senate, Locher, calculating that his political future lay with the so-called cosmo voters of Cleveland, returned to head the law department of Mayor Anthony Celebrezze, who had been put into city hall by Louis Seltzer, of the *Cleveland Press,* and the Cleveland cabal of the Cleveland Trust Company, the large corporations, and their law firms over the opposition of the Democratic party. Celebrezze later went on to become John F. Kennedy's Secretary of the new cabinet department of Health, Education, and Welfare. (There is a story, no doubt apocryphal, that Kennedy, concerned with the ethnic make-up of his cabinet, turned to an aide and said, "Get me that Italian in Ohio," meaning Michael V. DiSalle, then Ohio's governor, and got Mayor Anthony J. Celebrezze instead.) Celebrezze's cabinet service was followed by an appointment to the United States Court of Appeals.

In reply to Stokes's letter, Locher wrote:

Dear Carl:
    Acknowledging your recent letter of resignation, please be assured of our every good wish for you in your cam-

paign for nomination and election to the office of State Representative. I feel sure that your experience as an assistant Police Prosecutor will stand you in good stead throughout life and throughout your career as an attorney and in the course of public office which you will undoubtedly hold in the years to come.

Little did he realize that Carl would be sending his R.S.V.P. so soon.

4. THE LOSER

CARL STOKES had always been good at arithmetic. With Cleveland's Negro population exceeding 300,000 by 1960, it seemed about time for a Negro to be elected to some office other than city council or the municipal court, the only offices to which a Negro Democrat had ever been elected in Cleveland. He had already learned that municipal court was only the stepchild of Cleveland city government, and, furthermore, a judicial career did not appeal to his restless, activist nature.

Nor did city council hold any interest for him. For the last generation, Negroes have had no difficulty being elected to that body, primarily because there has been nothing the party leaders could do to prevent it. As the central city wards became more solidly Negro, so did their representation in council, and by 1960 there were ten Negro councilmen in Cleveland's thirty-three-man council. Though the county Democratic party was impotent in the mayor's office, it wielded great power and discipline in council (in which there are rarely more than two or three Republicans), and as of 1960, at least, it was almost impossible for a Negro councilman to exert any influence or power outside his own ward. Within his ward he was powerful enough—with control over zoning- and liquor-permit protests and the various perquisites that councilmen enjoy in most cities. But council was strictly a dead end for a Negro, and it was not what Stokes wanted.

He looked instead toward Columbus, where, under Ohio's apportionment system at that time, Cuyahoga County was entitled to seventeen representatives in the state house, all of whom were elected on an at-large basis throughout the county. Virtually all of Cleveland's Negroes are squeezed within the city limits, only a few residing in such suburbs as Lakewood, Shaker Heights, Cleveland Heights, Beachwood, Hunting Valley, Gates Mills, Pepper Pike, and others. And, with the exception of Shaker Heights, the only black faces to be seen in 1960 in most of those suburbs were in a kitchen or behind a rake in someone's yard.

So, the ratio of black to white was considerably decreased in a race for the state legislature with a county-wide population of 1,600,000. Nevertheless, with more than 75,000 registered Negro voters, and as few as 40,000 votes needed to assure nomination, one of those seventen seats looked ripe for the taking. He had tested the water briefly in 1958 right after law school, when he had filed nominating petitions for the Democratic primary for the state legislature. But he had done no more than pay his $50 filing fee, and finished far down the list of candidates. Now, however, he was ready to campaign as a serious candidate.

Prior to reapportionment of the Ohio legislature in 1965, leading to the creation of single member districts, nomination in the Democratic primary in Cuyahoga County was virtually tantamount to election, since the Democrats in the postwar years had almost always elected a solid delegation. Carl thought one of those seventeen seats had his name written on it, and he decided to run in the Democratic primary. (Never, at any time, has he considered running for office as a Republican. As noted, he is very good at arithmetic.)

Due to the at-large system of electing legislators, the primary was a mad scramble in which as many as one hundred candidates appeared on the ballot—called by its critics the "bedsheet ballot," with its confusing list of Irish, Polish, Hungarian, Slovakian, Italian, and sometimes even Anglo-Saxon names. This, of course, was a completely indigestible smorgasbord for the Democratic voter, and in hopeless confusion, he would usually select the seventeen dishes that had been pre-picked for him by the party. Which meant by Ray T. Miller, a politician of the Last Hurrah School who had ruled the Democratic party of Cuyahoga County firmly and autocratically since his one-term as mayor of Cleveland in the early thirties. Though he had virtually no influence in the mayor's office from the time of Frank Lausche (who had gained that post largely through Miller's support but who had later become Miller's political foe, like others before him—DiSalle, Celebrezze, Louis Seltzer) his power in city council, in county offices, and in the Cuyahoga County delegation to the state legislature was awesome.

Miller was the archetypal big-city political boss—a big, round, florid-faced Irishman with an overpowering and intimidating personality. He was a master technician at playing off factions within the city against each other, and at producing impressive county Democratic majorities in national elections. But he was never known to express an opinion on a controversial political issue, and if he had a political philosophy, it was a well-kept secret. His power was never seriously challenged, and local, state, even national politicians paid obeisance to it. He obtained a measure of national importance when he became the first big-city chairman to endorse John F. Kennedy at a time when it was not at all certain that Kennedy would win the nomination. Miller died in 1965, a year after his retirement as Democratic county chairman. With the tremendous power he exerted for thirty years—those same years that marked Cleveland's sad decline—he must share part of the blame for the city's present woes with those others equally influential who failed to wield that power for progressive change in Cleveland—the mayors, the banks, the newspapers, the corporations, the law firms, and the labor unions.

It was in the spring of 1960 when Carl Stokes, about to seek his first elective office as a loyal, dutiful Democrat, went to Ray Miller to ask for one of the seventeen legislative endorsements. The Cuyahoga County democratic organization had never endorsed a Negro for the state legislature, and no Negro Democrat from Cuyahoga County—in fact, from the entire state—had ever been elected to that august body. Stokes suggested that it was high time—one hundred years after the Thirteenth Amendment—Ohio had Negro Democratic representation in Columbus. While not particularly interested in constitutional arguments, Miller agreed to give Carl an endorsement. Stokes looked like a winner to him in any case, so it was better to keep him in the party fold.

With a large Negro vote, with the newspapers in his corner, and now with the party behind him, Carl felt assured of the nomination. Meanwhile, he could continue in his post as assistant prosecutor and do his campaigning on a part-time basis. Without ever having campaigned for office, he was already the best-known Negro politician in Cleveland. It began to seem possible that he might even lead the legislative ticket.

But what had proved so effective for white candidates appeared to be less so for a Negro candidate. Carl ran eighteenth in a field of fifty, losing the seventeenth spot to an unendorsed candidate with a white skin and a powerful name. William Feighan, son of Congressman Michael Feighan, won the nomination by two hundred votes, and, after a recount, was still the winner. There was, in fact, a double recount which reduced the margin of victory to just eight votes. Stokes was to have less than complete confidence in the vote-counting ability of the County Board of Elections as a result of this experience, and in 1967 his organization would provide witnesses for every one of the city's 903 precincts.

Carl had in fact received less than half of the Negro votes, and virtually none from whites. He had learned his first important political lesson. He would have to build his own power base among the Negroes to overcome the fragmentation that had been imposed on Negro wards to keep any single Negro politician from assuming too much power. Jealous of their own power within their wards, the Negro councilmen had given Stokes very little help in his campaign. By subtly encouraging these rivalries, the political parties in Cleveland had up to that time succeeded in limiting Negro political effectiveness. Negro voters, if not indifferent, were rarely given any reason to be enthusiastic about local elections beyond the ward borders. Accordingly, they had simply been unprepared for a man who was asking to represent all of them in Columbus, and not just a few thousand of them in council. Stokes had failed to get the message to them and no one else was about to do it.

Only one Negro councilman had ever attracted significant attention beyond his own ward—Leo Jackson—and he had accomplished that by a curious reversal of the police-brutality theme. Jackson claimed that the police were not arresting *enough* Negroes—that too many petty crimes were simply ignored by the police in Negro areas and that this in turn encouraged further Negro crime. This, of course, made good news copy, and has made Jackson Cleveland's best-known Negro councilman. But his law-enforcement theories are really more popular with white voters than with black, and not all Negroes like him. Leo Jackson is a brave, honest, hard-working officeholder, but he has a high-pitched, unattractive speaking voice and an unfortunate tendency to stammer under stress. It was not difficult for Carl Stokes, with his cool confidence, his friendly Pepsodent smile, and his electric platform style, to supplant Leo Jackson as Cleveland's best-known Negro politician.

Carl knew now that party endorsement alone wasn't enough to put him into office. He would have to make himself popular enough in the Negro wards to neutralize other Negro politicians. Form his own alliances, his own organization, his own coalitions. Oppose the party on particular issues when necessary—do anything, in short, that would make him a hero to every Negro voter in town. There would be time enough to go after the white votes later on.

5. THE LEGISLATOR

Bⁿ 1962 Carl Stokes had gone a long way toward reaching rung number one on his political ladder—a large, secure power base among the Negro voters. Resigning from the prosecutor's office, he was easily elected to the Ohio legislature and became the first Negro Democrat ever to sit in the Ohio house of representatives.

He sat but he did not sit still, and in that notably conservative body it was relatively easy for a man on the make to have an impact. The legislature, as it existed in

1962, was called the "corn-stalk brigade" because of its lopsided domination by rural representatives. In such company, a city slicker like Carl Stokes soon began to attract attention. Though his power as a first-term legislator was limited, his propensity for making news was not. He was grabbing the headlines from his fellow members, but he was making them like it.

A veteran Columbus legislative correspondent, observing the Stokes technique, described it this way for his newspapers:

> Another Stokes trait that smothers incipient resentment is his affable nature. In a body of peers where pride and prerogatives are constantly exposed, the opportunity for treading on both is always present. Yet Stokes has managed to tiptoe around wounded egos by letting others see him laugh at himself, by refusing to bear grudges against those who spear him, and by avoiding personality conflicts. He is slow to anger but quick to shake it off, once he simmers to a burn.

Carl made sure, of course, that all this news reached the right ears and in less than one year in his first elective office he was the undisputed political king of the east side. Now no Negro politician would dare challenge him, and though some would refuse to openly support him, they could not afford to oppose him.

Only one other Negro officeholder at that time could have seriously challenged Carl Stokes in public esteem and regard. Merle McCurdy, a handsome, forceful, articulate man, had been one of Cleveland's best trial lawyers as an assistant county prosecutor, until his appointment by President Kennedy as United States Attorney—a post he administered so well that many urged him to run for elective office. Since McCurdy and Stokes were not rivals, it was easy for them to become friends and allies, though McCurdy's political support was circumscribed by his government position.

In November 1967 McCurdy took a leave of absence from his post to become the general counsel of the President's riot commission (officially and euphemistically called Commission on Civil Disorders). Accordingly, both Stokes and McCurdy, two local boys who made it, had a great deal to say about the future of America's cities. Merle McCurdy was well on the way to becoming a national figure of some importance when his career was tragically ended by a brain hemorrhage from which he died in May 1968 at the age of fifty-five.

Not only had Stokes solidified and enlarged his Negro support; he had also won the hearts of Cuyahoga County's white liberal voters, who did not often find heroes among Cleveland legislators. Carl had long been a member of Americans for Democratic Action, but that organization represented only a small fraction of the county's liberal vote. In fact, ADA in Ohio was about as effective as its arch enemy, the John Birch Society. Each organization had small but loyal and dedicated (fanatic, each would say of the other) memberships, and spent a great deal of time attacking the other. Needless to say, neither group had much impact on elections. But Carl no longer had to depend on the limited ADA membership: true love was beginning to bloom between him and the county's white liberals. That love would be put to a severe test on several occasions in the years to come.

Unfortunately, all but a few of those white liberal supporters lived outside the city, and though they were now his state-legislature constituents, they could be of no help (except as campaign workers and financial supporters) in a mayoral race. And so, though he was immeasurably stronger on a county-wide basis, his city voting strength was still weak, and he was not yet ready to attack city hall.

He had watched with great interest from the state house in Columbus, while his boss from his prosecutor days, Ralph Locher, succeeded Anthony Celebrezze as mayor when the latter assumed his post in President Kennedy's cabinet. Locher had been re-elected without opposition to a full two-year term in 1963, but was beginning to be treated unkindly by the newspapers, and, as was typical of Cleveland mayors, was on poor terms with the Democratic party organization. Neither of these circumstances was of much comfort to Stokes, who knew that the newspapers had always been rough with mayors in mid-term just to show them who was boss (while editorializing against political bossism), only to support them at re-election time, and he knew that no matter how bitter the feelings between Albert Porter, the new Democratic county chairman, and Ralph Locher, the one thing that would send them flying into each other's arms would be Carl Stokes's entry into the Democratic mayoral primary.

So city hall would have to wait. Meanwhile, though Carl knew he could easily be re-elected to the legislature in 1964, he did not look forward to another term in Columbus. He was too restless and result-oriented for the slow process of legislative work, much of it dealing with matters of no importance to him. The rurally dominated Ohio legislature was almost totally indifferent to urban problems, which, of course, were his main interest. Also while the legislature gave him good exposure and enabled him to form valuable alliances, as a junior member of the minority party (or, in a way, the junior member of two minority parties, since he was outranked by the other two Negroes in Ohio's 134-man house), he had virtually no influence over legislation.

Furthermore, the pay was low ($8,000 a year), and the work kept him away from his family too long. In 1958 Carl had married a Mississippi girl named Shirley Edwards, a graduate of Fisk University, and now had two children—Carl, Jr., born in 1959, and a daughter, Cordi, born in 1961.

Carl had been married once before. In fact, twice, to the same girl, but whatever the difficulty of the first marriage, it was not cured by the second, and so Carl had been married and divorced twice before he was thirty—the only fact in his personal background that conflicted with the image of a perfect politician.

Shirley Stokes is a lovely, gracious woman of thirty, who has a shyness about her, and an air of vulnerability that makes people want to be protective of her. She is unwilling to make speeches to large gatherings, and though she hates campaigning, she performs her role with grace and charm.

It is her complete lack of guile that has on occasion led her to make certain awkward (politically, that is) remarks, such as the time she was asked why her son went to a suburban private school when the city of which her husband was trying to become mayor maintained a school just a few short blocks from her home. With all candor she replied that the school in their neighborhood couldn't offer their son a good education.

From the time Carl Stokes began to attain political prominence, Shirley Stokes has been deluged by obscene telephone calls and poison-pen letters, which she has suffered with patience and dignity; but she still trembles when the phone rings late at night if Carl is not home. It is painful to think of this sweet and gentle woman picking up the telephone and waiting to see if it will be her husband's voice or, once again, those ugly, hate-filled words, "you dirty nigger."

There would certainly be fewer nights at home alone for Shirley and the children, Carl thought, if he passed up the next chance for re-election. Besides, he had for several years been in partnership with his brother Louis in the law firm of Stokes and Stokes, and if he were able to spend full time in the practice, it would be less of a burden on Lou and both of them could make more money. Louis Stokes is Carl's best friend, and perhaps the only person who really knows Carl Stokes, the man, when he has stepped out of the image of Carl Stokes, the politician. Lou has stayed unobtrusively in the background and watched his brother skyrocket to fame, but when Carl really wants to talk to someone, it is Lou he seeks out.

Lou had already established a reputation as one of Cleveland's most able lawyers, and, in addition to maintaining a busy practice, had found the time to handle or direct much of the NAACP litigation in the area. There is no doubt that if Carl, himself a first-rate lawyer, had chosen to practice full time, the firm of Stokes and Stokes could have become eminently successful.

Perhaps, Carl reasoned, the thing to do was stay in Cleveland, keep one eye on city hall, and be ready to storm it the moment it seemed accessible. Locher's mistakes had already formed a drawbridge halfway across the moat. But Carl had political momentum going, and he was reluctant to lose it by dropping out of the public eye, even temporarily.

There was one other possibility, which would keep him out of Columbus but in public office, and one infinitely more exciting than the state legislature. Charles Vanik had parlayed a Slovenian background, a handsome face, and a quick wit into a successful congressional career. He had served five terms as representative to Congress from Cleveland's Twenty-first Congressional District, which, when he had first been elected, had been a solid nationality district but which had gradually changed its composition and color, being almost 50 per cent Negro by 1964. It was the district in which Carl lived, and he knew that with Vanik out of the way, he would have an excellent chance to win that seat. Vanik, eight years earlier, before he began to enjoy the comforts of congressional seniority, had wanted to run against Mayor Celebrezze in the Democratic primary. The party, as usual, was feuding with city hall, but Ray Miller refused to commit it to an endorsement, and Vanik had stayed in Congress. It is likely that Vanik, who has always been popular with Cleveland voters, could have beaten Celebrezze, thus nipping in the bud that spectacular career that led to the cabinet and the United States Court of Appeals, and, in turn, scotching the career of Anthony Calabrese, a complete unknown who had made it in the Ohio legislature simply because his name sounded like Celebrezze, as did that of his son, Anthony Jr. There have since been other Celebrezzes elected to office in Cleveland, but by this time no one knows if it's because their names sound like Celebrezze or like Calabrese.

A man like Carl Stokes was doubly disadvantaged in such a system. With a different color and a different name, he would have to run on his own merits: he could never be elected by voters who thought they were voting for someone else.

Like many others at this time, Carl was convinced that Vanik could easily defeat Locher in the Democratic primary for mayor in 1965; and in fact Vanik was being urged to run. But, though he had coveted the job years before, he was no longer willing to surrender valuable seniority in Congress, though he knew he might have to do that anyway should Carl Stokes decide to challenge him in the congressional primary. Vanik was popular with both black and white voters, but he could not hope to match Carl's popularity with Negro voters, and they now composed almost half of his district.

Carl weighed the possibilities. He was sure he could have as big an impact in the big leagues in Washington as he had had in the minors in Columbus. But he was not so sure that he would be elected. The Negroes in his district were used to voting for Vanik, and he would have to wage a full-scale campaign to beat him. It would be difficult to raise money for a race against this man who had made so many friends and so few enemies; and losing the race might kill his political career. Furthermore, he liked Charley Vanik—he would be a good one to keep in his corner. All things considered, then, it seemed unwise to run—at least now—so Vanik, with the field to himself, heaved a sigh of relief and went back to Washington.

The shortest route to city hall was by way of Columbus after all . . .

6. OUT OF ORBIT

THOUGH Carl returned to Columbus for another two-year term as a result of the November 1964 elections, his heart lay elsewhere. His attendance record was one of the poorest in the entire house, and he was publicly criticized for not minding the store. Yet, his political magic had become so effective by this time that he emerged from the session a much more powerful political figure than when he had entered it.

United States Supreme Court decisions in 1964 called for the redistricting of Ohio's congressional districts and the reapportionment of its state legislative districts, the former to be accomplished by an act of the Ohio legislature, the latter by an amendment to the Ohio constitution, to be voted on by the people in the May 1965 primary election. Both were to have an impact on Stokes's political career.

In spite of the fact that Cuyahoga County was overwhelmingly Democratic, skillful gerrymandering by Ohio's Republican legislatures had kept Cleveland's four-seat congressional delegation equally divided between the parties. Though there was little chance of any bill out of Columbus upsetting this balance, Carl thought that the judicial decisions might alter the racial imbalance in Cleveland's congressional districts and, incidentally, gain him a congressional seat. He was therefore an interested observer and a behind-the-scenes participant as his brother Lou and a committee of NAACP lawyers prepared to file a law suit challenging the constitutionality of the new districting bill.

Meanwhile, his friend, Congressman Vanik, had his own ideas about congressional redistricting, and had his staff draft a redistricting bill that would make his own seat more secure but, at the same time, dilute the Negro congressional voting strength, thus postponing for perhaps a few more years the possibility of a Negro congressman from Cleveland. Such a bill, of course, was hardly calculated to win Vanik any new Negro support, and he could not afford to be publicly associated with it. He therefore had his bill presented to the Ohio legislature by someone with whom he could not be identified. It came to nothing. The NAACP law suit, however, was more successful; the Supreme Court has ordered new congressional districts for Ohio, which may well help send a Negro from Cleveland to Congress. The name of the first Negro congressman will most likely be Stokes; but it will be Louis, not Carl, since the mayor's brother has become the Democratic candidate in the new district.

One other short chapter of Ohio's bizarre political history indirectly affected the career of Carl Stokes in 1964 —more for what he did not do than for what he did. In early 1964 Colonel John Glenn, America's first space hero, decided to challenge Senator Stephen Young in the May 1964 Democratic primary. Young had been a loyal and trusted officeholder for most of the past fifty years, but in 1964 he was already past seventy and his Republican opponent in the fall would be Robert Taft, Jr., son of *the* Robert Taft, a name that strikes terror in the hearts of all Ohio Democrats. Taft looked like a sure winner and Young a sure loser. Then America's most famous man, Colonel John Glenn, came blasting into Ohio's political scene, with retro rockets going full power, and the Democrats seemed certain to retain the Senate seat. But they were not happy. Steve Young had collected a lot of IOU's in that half-century of service, and he began to cash them in at a furious rate. Very few Democrats of any prominence dared to express public support of Glenn, though of course none, save Steve Young himself, dared to knock him. Nothing so depresses a politician as being forced into a position of supporting a loser, and no Ohio Democrat was singing "Happy Days Are Here Again."

Meanwhile, Glenn, whose platform was still top secret, being hidden behind a cloak of Marine regulations prohibiting political activity, and who had taken no political action beyond announcing his candidacy and filing his petitions for the May primary, was having great difficulty recruiting a campaign organization. Six amateur Cleveland politicians finally agreed to form a campaign committee if they could be informed as to the candidate's views and programs, and so a secret meeting was held in February 1964 in the Marriott Motel in Washington, D.C., at which Glenn tried to answer all the questions put to him by his potential political cadre. They were pleasantly surprised: instead of finding the traditional conservative military mind, they found a well-informed middle-of-the-roader who expressed some opinions that would have pleased even the ADA. He thought, for example, that the election of Barry Goldwater would be a national disaster, and that international atomic and arms control was an absolute necessity.

The Clevelanders agreed to support Glenn, and hurried back home to recruit an organization. One of the first people they approached was Cleveland's most promising Democrat. But Carl Stokes faced the same dilemma as other Democrats. While Glenn had a better chance of beating Taft, Carl didn't feel secure enough to risk opposing a party wheel-horse like Steve Young. Nor could he afford to alienate Howard Metzenbaum, a Cleveland lawyer and business tycoon who was Young's friend and adviser and who could always be counted on to raise prodigious sums of money for political campaigns. He had, for example, raised a $100,000 campaign fund just the year before with a Steve Young appreciation dinner. (This was, of course, a pre-Dodd dinner.)

So Carl said no thanks to the Glenn people, but he was luckier than the other Democrats. He had a brother Lou and they didn't, and Carl had no objection to Lou's taking part in the Glenn campaign. Thus Carl found himself in that happy state coveted by all politicians: he had maneuverability no matter who won.

As it turned out, neither Louis Stokes nor anyone else did much campaigning for John Glenn, who, as the world knows, was forced to withdraw from the race because of injuries suffered in a fall. And so, the political career of the first American to orbit the earth was wiped out in a crash landing in a Columbus, Ohio, bathroom, and Steve Young was swept back into office, to the amazement of most, in the Johnson landslide of 1964. Young had won his first victory over another Ohio Republican hero, John Bricker, by the massive Democratic vote that labor had turned out to defeat a right-to-work proposal on the Ohio ballot in 1958.

Steve Young carefully noted the names of those who had taken part in the Glenn campaign, and later helped to block a federal appointment for one of them. By staying on the sidelines, Carl Stokes, on the other hand, had cemented his relationship with the Senator, who was to remember it later.

7. THE MAVERICK

THE ISSUE of state legislative apportionment almost caused a divorce between Carl Stokes and his white liberal supporters, but as it turned out, it was just a lovers' quarrel, the first of several they were to have.

In 1964, the dead hand of Mark Hanna, probably the most powerful political boss Ohio has ever had, still determined the make-up of the Ohio house of representatives. In 1903, to insure his own re-election as a United States senator, Hanna had traded an Ohio constitutional amendment for votes of rural Ohio state legislators (at that time state legislatures elected senators). That amendment, ever since known as the Hanna amendment, guaranteed each of Ohio's eighty-eight counties, regardless of size, at least one member in the Ohio house. Since there was a built-in limitation on the number of representatives from large counties, and as the population shifted from rural to urban, by 1960 the house was controlled by less than 30 per cent of the population. This meant urban under-representation, which in turn meant Democratic under-representation, and under-representation of Ohio's Negroes, most of whom were city residents.

When the Supreme Court struck down the Hanna amendment, the Democratic party of Ohio licked its lips in anticipation of finally tasting the majority representation its numbers deserved. But in the Columbus state house sat a crafty Republican politician who was to snatch that juicy morsel from the Democrats' hands before it ever reached their lips. James A. Rhodes had succeeded Governor Michael V. DiSalle in a bitter campaign in 1962 which left both men holding grudges against each other. Never had two such contrasting public figures served successive terms as governor.

Mike DiSalle is a New Deal Democrat who believed it his duty as governor to bring Ohio, kicking and screaming if necessary, into the twentieth century. He thought it an anomaly no longer to be tolerated for Ohio, among the leading states in wealth and industrial might, to rank near the bottom in education and welfare expenditures. Rhodes, on the other hand, is a McKinley Republican who believes that if business is good, everything else will be good—a philosophy embodied in his slogan: "Profit is not a dirty word in Ohio."

DiSalle suspected that Rhodes had exended his profit motive a little too far, and accused him, not only of having used campaign funds for personal use, but also of income-tax evasion on those funds. The accusation was never completely proved or disproved, but the voters of Ohio did not particularly care. They preferred Jim Rhodes's cheer-leading to Mike DiSalle's scolding.

DiSalle made the fatal political mistake of trying to govern Ohio according to the dictates of his conscience. He thought Ohio's welfare system was a disgrace and said so. He tried to shame Ohioans into modernizing the state's inadequate educational system. He was sickened by the deplorable condition of state mental institutions, and proposed increased taxes to remedy these and other ills. He thought it an abomination for the state to execute human beings, and he commuted death penalties and spoke and wrote against capital punishment. He attended very few ceremonial functions, believing it far more important to attend to work in Columbus.

Increased taxes is never a popular program on which to run for re-election, and there are no votes on death row. DiSalle could not match the super salesmanship of Rhodes, and was decisively defeated. Today, James Rhodes dashes around the state, the country, and the world with all the razz ma tazz of Harold Hill, mostly extolling the virtues of Ohio tomato juice. No one seems to notice that little else is being accomplished on the state government level. He is a powerful man, however, with a clever political machine, trying to maneuver for a spot on the Republican national ticket in 1968. Tomato juice can be a strong drink.

It is a measure of Carl Stokes's adaptability that he is on excellent terms with both Mike DiSalle and Jim Rhodes. No one else in Ohio can make that statement. Stokes and DiSalle had known each other for years, and when Carl was to call upon that friendship later for help in the Taft campaign, DiSalle would respond immediately and eloquently. Stokes first earned the gratitude of Jim Rhodes in the reapportionment issue of 1965, though Carl's position on that issue was taken without regard to Rhodes but for motives of his own. With his knack for turning near-disaster into triumph, Jim Rhodes devised an apportionment plan to subdistrict the large counties, so that no longer could the urban areas expect to send top-heavy democratic delegations to Columbus. Thus, loss of rural Republican representation would be more than offset by that from the cities. Subdistricting had long been desired by good-government groups in Ohio, and so organizations like the League of Women Voters and the Citizens' League were willing to overlook some basic and dangerous defects in the Rhodes plan for the opportunity to do away with the bedsheet ballot. Never mind the fact that the bill was a wide-open invitation to gerrymandering, or that it gave unlimited freedom of discretion to power-hungry politicians; what they wanted most of all was smaller legislative districts, and that the bill provided.

There was immediate opposition to the plan, however, which was to be voted in the May 1965 primary. The labor unions, the Democrats, the ADA, the political-science professors all took dead aim at issue Number 3, as the proposal was to be designated on the ballot. But Carl Stokes was not on the firing line with them. His seat in the legislature was secure regardless of how it was apportioned, but he never really had a choice on the issue; he would be forced to campaign for it no matter what it might cost him in party, and labor, and liberal esteem; the fact was, issue 3 would lead to more Negro legislators from Cleveland. Subdistricting meant the creation of three or more legislative districts with predominantly Negro populations, and instead of just Carl Stokes in Columbus to represent 300,000 Negroes, they would have representation more in proportion to their numbers. This was being patiently explained to them nearly every week in the pages of the *Call and Post,* a Cleveland weekly published primarily for Negro readers by a Negro Republican, William O. Walker, who had been appointed by Governor Rhodes as his director of industrial relations, a job that left Walker with plenty of time to try to cultivate Negro votes for Rhodes.

How could a Negro politician possibly take a stand against issue 3 when the argument for it was so simple—more Negro legislators—and the argument against it so sophisticated, subtle, and scientific? Already there were rumblings by black nationalists and Negro militants to the effect that Carl Stokes was no better than a white liberal with a black face. How could he risk losing a substantial number of Negroes to the militants or the hotheads? And so Carl Stokes campaigned for issue 3. The Democrats shouted maverick, the labor leaders fumed, and the ADA shed a tear. But James Rhodes and William Walker were pleased, and a great deal of attention began to be given to the career of Carl Stokes in the pages of the *Call and Post*.

ADA could hardly wait to kiss and make up. In February 1965, at the City Club in Cleveland, Stokes debated issue 3 before an ADA audience, taking the pro side (that is, the Rhodes-Walker side) while Frank King, state chairman of the AFL-CIO, and state senate minority leader, spoke for the opposition. Though the audience clearly sympathized with King's arguments, the *man* they liked was Carl Stokes. His charm and wit could not be matched on the platform by Frank King—as they would not be matched by Seth Taft two years later.

In spite of the best efforts of Jim Rhodes, William Walker, and Carl Stokes, however, issue 3 was defeated in the May primary, and labor and the Democrats thought they had won. But Democrats hardly ever win in Ohio, and the federal court imposed its own plan of apportionment, which was in effect quite similar to the one Jim Rhodes wanted in the first place. It is still Ohio's apportionment system, and there *are* more Negroes in the legislature, and Carl Stokes's power base could not be more secure.

8. THE INDEPENDENT

SUDDENLY and unexpectedly, in the spring of 1965, city hall, which had still seemed many years away in 1964, loomed up almost within reach. Ralph Perk, the Cuyahoga County auditor and the only Republican to have held that office, or any other non-judicial county office, for twenty years, became the Republican candidate for mayor. This was the first time in many years that a proven Republican vote-getter had dared run for mayor of Cleveland, where in 1960 there were only approximately 35,000 registered

Republicans out of a total of 325,000 voters. (Of this total, only 170,000 were registered as Democrats, but of the balance of 120,000 registered voters who did not vote in primary elections and thus carried no party designation in the poll books, almost 100,000 generally voted Democratic.) Those were tough odds to beat, and only someone desperately anxious to see his name on a ballot would offer himself up as the sacrificial Republican candidate. There had actually been no Republican candidate in 1963, and Ralph Locher had run unopposed. But criticism of him had been growing more and more intense and Cleveland, the slumbering giant, was beginning to awaken from its twenty-year sleep to learn that the rest of the country was passing it by. Locher began to be criticized even for things that should have been done by Lausche and Burke and Celebrezze. But, of course, they had not been done by Locher, either.

The Republicans saw an opportunity to recapture city hall for the first time since the late thirties administration of Edward Blythin, who later was to achieve fame, of a sort, as the judge in the well-publicized (overpublicized, according to the Supreme Court) Dr. Sam Sheppard murder case. So they persuaded their best vote-getter, Ralph Perk, to run for mayor (risking only his prestige and not his job, since he could make the race without resigning as county auditor). Perk, a former councilman with a solid cosmo voting base, had scored a major upset just a few years previously by turning out of office the perennial county auditor, Democrat John Carney, of the rich and politically powerful Carney family.

What gave Stokes reason to hope was the provision in the Cleveland city charter which permitted independent candidates for mayor to run in the general election against the party candidates. Stokes knew that he would lose in a primary race against Locher, because his white supporters (with the exception of those egghead types who lived in the University Circle area) were virtually all suburbanites, ineligible to vote in the Cleveland mayoral race, and the white vote in Cleveland exceeded the Negro vote by almost two to one no matter how it was counted.

But if Ralph Perk could exploit the dissatisfaction with Locher and draw a substantial portion of his votes, and if Carl Stokes could get a solid bloc of 100,000 Negro votes, then maybe, just maybe—the arithmetic began to look good.

Then something happened which settled all doubts in Carl's mind and convinced him that he would be elected mayor of Cleveland in 1965. Another candidate entered the race—one who came to the people's attention through the highly charged issue of urban public education. Ralph McAllister was a new phenomenon in city politics—the beneficiary, or victim, of the passions that engulf the problem of de facto segregation in city schools. This new breed of urban politician was to reach its fullest development two years later in Boston, Massachusetts, in the ample form of a lady named Louise Day Hicks.

In 1967, Mrs. Hicks led a field of nine mayoral candidates in Boston's non-partisan primary. Mrs. Hicks believes in the neighborhood school system and is against busing of school children for desegregation purposes. No one has been able to determine what else, if anything, she is for or against. No one seems to care; she led the ticket.

Every city has its Louise Day Hicks. Cleveland's in 1965 was Ralph McAllister, a tall, stern, sullen forty-year-old lawyer. McAllister had started his political career in the same manner as Carl Stokes—by running for and losing a Democratic nomination to the state legislature in 1960. Two years later he had been elected to the Cleveland Board of Education, and by 1964 had become president of the board. Almost without realizing what was happening, he suddenly became a champion of the neighborhood school system and a hero to the nervous whites in neighborhoods bordering the Negro areas who feared that "they" were about to overrun the schools. McAllister would save their neighborhoods. He knew how to stand up to "them" and how to keep "them" in their place.

In April 1964 a group of black and white demonstrators opposing the construction of what they claimed was an inadequate and improperly located school in a Negro neighborhood staged a sit-in to impede work on the building. In the confusion a young white Protestant minister named Bruce Klunder was killed when a bulldozer accidentally backed over him. Reverend Klunder became a martyr to the school segregation fight in Cleveland, and emotions and tensions swirled about the head of Ralph McAllister. A man of little imagination and rigid morality, he was loudly encouraged by a small but enthusiastic band of right-wingers who saw a leader in him. Misled by their enthusiasm, McAllister determined to run for mayor as an independent candidate in 1965. *INDEPENDENT*

Both Stokes and McAllister filed nominating petitions in July 1965 with over twelve thousand signatures, enough to place them on the November ballot, alongside Ralph Perk and Ralph Locher, who were certain to win the party primaries in October. As it turned out, Locher's victory was in the balance, since he won by only six thousand votes over county recorder Mark McElroy. McElroy was popular but not *that* popular, and the close primary was more a vote against Locher and a portent of things to come. The Democratic party, never close to Locher, had endorsed McElroy, but, after Locher's victory, suddenly found virtues in him that had not been apparent before.

Now that there was a three-way split, Stokes thought he had an even better chance of winning. If as many as 200,000 white voters were to turn out (which was more than usually voted in a mayoral race), it seemed unlikely that Locher could receive enough support to offset Stokes's Negro bloc. Neither of the other candidates had much prospect of getting more than fifty thousand votes each.

Following a basic rule of politics—campaigning where the votes are—Stokes planned to concentrate his efforts on the east side to bring out as large a Negro vote as possible. He had neither the staff nor the funds to do much more. His loyal ADA friends formed a hard-working cadre for him, and volunteers turned out in large numbers. Young people have always been attracted to

Stokes, and college students flocked to the second-floor downtown headquarters he had opened; but the campaign lacked professional leadership and organization, and, to a large extent, the volunteers simply got in each other's way.

As for his major opposition, Ralph Locher, the year 1965 had been a bad one. In January, James Stanton, the new young president of city council and a man many were boosting as Cleveland's next mayor, had called for new leadership at city hall. In April, Democratic chairman Albert Porter publicly criticized Locher, accusing him of never having been an organization Democrat. Even if Locher was not ready to sing his swan song, it began to look as though the party was going to sing it for him.

But not only was he in trouble with the party. The Negro community, which had centered its hostility on Ralph McAllister as the symbol of reaction and repression, began to transfer at least part of that bitterness to the more benign figure of Ralph Locher, mainly over an issue that concerned his police chief, Richard Wagner, a man they resented even more than McAllister. Wagner had testified before the state legislature in opposition to a capital-punishment abolition bill. Ordinarily such activity by a law-enforcement official would have received only passing notice by the general community, but Wagner had advanced the most novel reason yet heard for the retention of the death penalty: he claimed that abolition would promote black nationalism and that, in effect, society needed capital punishment for the protection of innocent whites against vengeful blacks. This was too much for Cleveland's Negroes, who, while they had come to expect the worst from Chief Wagner, were outraged by this strange testimony.

The United Freedom Movement, a civil-rights organization that had been created in the wake of Cleveland's school segregation fight, dispatched a delegation to city hall to insist that the mayor order the chief to retract or explain his weird remarks. The mayor refused to see them all summer, and by the end of summer Locher had replaced McAllister as the focus of Negro resentment. At the same time, he had also replaced him as the white hope (though McAllister had filed nominating petitions with fifty thousand signatures, less than half of those signers would later vote for him in the election), and, having no record of accomplishment to run on, he campaigned as the man who "would not be pushed around" and as "the candidate of *all* the people" (meaning all the *white* people).

Banging the lectern, he would say defiantly, "When they picket my home and when they drop the dead rats on the city hall steps and when they demand to meet with me, in my judgment any mayor worthy of his salt would say: 'You go through regular channels and then I'll see you.' That's still my position."

To which Carl Stokes would respond: "The very essence of government reflects pressure from all sorts of divergent groups. The question is how best, with those pressures, to do what is in the best interest of all the people. A hard-nosed, podium-pounding attitude isn't helping any."

No one could quarrel with that, and the consensus of newspaper opinion of Locher in 1965 seemed to be reflected in Stokes's further statement: "Cleveland, under the mayor's sluggish custodial-type administration, is not only not finding the right answers to our municipal needs —it isn't even asking the right questions."

But, while the newspapers generously praised Stokes's record and abilities and potential, and continued to question Locher's, in the end both papers endorsed Locher, as they had in his last three campaigns, even though they were hard put to justify their decision. The Cleveland *Plain Dealer,* for example, had to fall back on honesty and clean living. "Ralph Locher as a man and as a public official is the essence of honesty. He and his record are impeccably clean." The editorial then went on to praise Cleveland's inexpensive garbage collection. (It sometimes seems that if race doesn't bring down the cities, garbage will.) The only suggestion that things might be less than perfect in Cleveland was the hope implicit in the statement that Ralph Locher was "the consensus candidate, the unifying candidate . . ." meaning, presumably, that there were more whites to be offended by Stokes's election than Negroes to resent Locher's election.

Too late Carl realized that he should have spent more time trying to reach white voters. At the traditional City Club candidates' debate, held on the Saturday preceding the election, he understood, perhaps for the first time, that he need no longer campaign as a Negro candidate, that Carl Stokes, the man, could reach any person of goodwill of whatever color.

The Cleveland-Sheraton Hotel's ballroom on that Saturday in November 1965 was packed with several thousand of the county's most aware citizens, black and white. All four candidates were on the platform, and it had been the only joint appearance of the campaign. Carl was at his best that day—urbane, articulate, informed, relaxed, confident—and dominated the meeting. It was perhaps the day Cleveland really became aware that Carl Stokes was a man to be reckoned with.

Unfortunately, elections are not won at the City Club. Labor, remembering Stokes's position on issue 3, opposed him. The Democratic party barred him from their meetings on the ground that he was an independent, not a Democrat. But what hurt most of all, and what probably cost him the election, was a whispering campaign calculated to exploit the fears and prejudices of apprehensive whites who had nervously observed tensions increasing between blacks and whites, not only in Cleveland but throughout the country. The Watts riot in Los Angeles had occurred only three months earlier, and now it was being passed around the white wards that "a vote for McAllister or Perk is a vote for the nigger." Whispering campaigns are always hard to track down, but Carl was convinced that this was partly the work of Bronis Klementowicz, Ralph Locher's law director, who took a leave of absence from his official post every two years to manage Locher's re-election campaigns. Though Klem, a dapper, conspiratorial man whose trademark is a cigarette holder which he uses to punctuate his remarks, was known as a political mastermind around city hall, his type of campaigning is becoming obsolete. The winds of change have finally reached Cleveland.

But the whispering technique was good for one last gasp in 1965. Stokes suspected that some of the whispers came from the AFL-CIO, and accused them of using racist techniques by notifying their members that Ralph Locher was the only "safe" candidate.

"This McCarthy-like mud-slinging," Stokes said, "this racist attack is in full keeping with the racist campaign that Patrick J. O'Malley [president of the Cleveland AFL-CIO] and his cohorts have been waging against me in the west side. I deplore this kind of un-American talk."

O'Malley explained that "safe" meant only safe for labor and did a little attacking of his own: "Stokes is the puppet of Republican schemers. Their names are Governor James Rhodes and his cabinet member, State Industrial Relations Director William O. Walker."

The voters, in the end, agreed that Locher was not only honest and clean; he was also safe. Thus he proved to be the winner once again with 87,833 votes to 85,375 for Stokes. (Perk received 41,109 and McAllister only 22,660.)

Carl Stokes now knew exactly what he had to do to win in 1967. In the next two years he would have to see, face to face, as many white people as possible. If they had a chance to talk to him, there would be no need to whisper about him. He would also need a more professional campaign staff and money enough for television appearances. Finally, he would have to see that every Negro who was eligible to vote was registered.

While Ralph Locher began to plod his way through what were to be his last two years in office, Carl Stokes began to plan for the campaign that would remove Locher from that office.

9. THE DEMOCRAT

S TOKES suddenly found himself famous. His near-election excited the curiosity of Negro and white groups throughout the country, and he was deluged with speaking engagements. The Ohio legislature had concluded its session in the summer of 1965, and for the balance of that year and much of 1966 he spent a good deal of his time on speaking tours. In 1966 he ran for his third term in the legislature and was easily elected.

Meanwhile, the trouble had finally come to Cleveland. In July 1966, only nine months after the re-election of Ralph Locher, "the unifying candidate," the city was torn apart by the Hough riots—four days and nights of terror and destruction that left Cleveland a bewildered and directionless city. In the streets of Hough, day and night, was Carl Stokes, dodging bullets, bottles, and bricks along with the police and the national guard until finally the nightmare was over.

More committees were formed, more commissions were set up to study the problem—but in the summer of 1967 the scars of Hough were still visible, and the city was still locked in a paralysis of inaction. It did indeed appear that Cleveland was "swiftly submerging under the accumulated weight of its many intractable problems."

Federal urban-renewal funds were withdrawn from the city because of its lagging program. Locher continued to quarrel with representatives of the Negro community, and was also quarreling with the business community. He had charged a committee of businessmen whose advice he had sought with being "politically motivated" when their advice proved to be critical of his administration. He refused help proffered by the Cleveland Bar Association to assist in clearing up the backlog of urban-renewal paperwork, and everywhere were whispers, threats, fears, and predictions of another long, hot summer in 1967, only longer and hotter.

Stokes, remembering what white fears of racial violence had done to his mayoral chances in 1965, quickly became a sponsor of legislation permitting more rapid mobilization of the Ohio national guard to cope with urban riots, and began to talk a great deal about law and order in the streets.

This, of course, was a much more conservative stance than he had adopted in his previous terms in the legislature. One reporter in the 1965 session had written that Stokes ". . . had a laudable interest in welfare and criminal-code legislation, but appeared concerned most of the time, however, with matters relating to the fight for equal treatment and equal opportunity for Negroes—a desirable goal but not the only one."

The switch in emphasis to a law-and-order theme came as a surprise to his liberal supporters. Law and order had champions enough: they expected him to fight for less popular causes. But Carl would disappoint them even more before terminating his legislative career.

Governor Rhodes had proposed a constitutional amendment that called for an appointive body, to be known as the Ohio Bond Commission, to authorize the issuance of bonds for capital-improvement purposes. To the Democrats and to labor, it looked like a gigantic boondoggle. To Rhodes, it was a way of providing needed funds without reneging on his campaign promise of "no new taxes." And to Carl Stokes, it meant the money needed, for example, by Cleveland State University, which in turn would help revitalize downtown Cleveland. In addition, there was the incidental benefit that his support of OBC, as it was known, would once again earn him the gratitude of Governor Rhodes and William Walker, who was still in the cabinet and still the publisher of the *Call and Post*.

The OBC proposal had strong editorial support, and, perhaps most important, powerful advocates in the business and banking communities. But the Democrats and the ADA bitterly opposed OBC, ostensibly on the grounds that it was an unsound and expensive way to finance public projects and that too much authority would be given to an appointive body that could operate outside legislative control. The wording of the proposal, as it was to appear on the ballot, was so complex as to make it difficult for the voter to know what he was voting for or against. The Governor was waging an all-out campaign for passage of the proposal, and it was on this issue that the state Democratic party saw an opportunity to effect his first major political setback.

The state Democratic organization, which for many years had been virtually nonexistent, had recently appointed a new director, Pete O'Grady, who was looking for just such a chance to give the party a victory over Rhodes. Under O'Grady's skillful leadership, state Democratic headquarters was beginning to show signs of life, and the word went out that every Democrat should oppose OBC. But Carl Stokes once again fought the party and his old friends in ADA, and campaigned strongly for OBC—which was being pushed strongly by the *Call and Post,* the *Plain Dealer,* and the *Press*. Carl's name often figured in the OBC stories, and the additional publicity in a mayoralty election year did him no harm.

The OBC proposal was voted down, however, in May 1967, and Jim Rhodes's prestige suffered a serious blow. State Democratic headquarters had its first important victory in years, and even the ADA began to flex its muscles. Ordinarily, a politician who bucks his party on two vital issues in the space of two years can expect some erosion of support, but Carl Stokes is no ordinary politician, and even though the issues he supported had been defeated, he emerged stronger than ever—not only with his old support, but with new alliances as well.

The national Democratic administration in Washington had long been aware of Carl Stokes, and now that 1967 looked like the year in which he would become a nationally important figure, Washington began to sit up and pay close attention. Democratic national headquarters desperately needed a Negro to win back that portion of Negro support which the party felt it was almost sure to lose to the Republicans in 1968 because of the presence in their ranks of Senator Edward Brooke of Massachusetts, the first Negro senator since reconstruction days. Brooke was potent political medicine. The Republicans had bottled the medicine and were peddling it around the country. It was selling well. The Democrats had nothing like that on their shelves to sell to the voters. All they had in that line of goods was an overstock of Adam Clayton Powell, and they couldn't even get that off their hands.

And then along came Carl Stokes, from that most unlikely of places—Cleveland, Ohio. How the Washington

Democrats welcomed him. He was even a better Negro than Ed Brooke. He was darker. He was *unmistakably* a Negro; he even had a Negro wife. There was only one drawback: he had run on an independent ticket in 1965 and there was every indication that he would do so again in 1967. It was already clear that Seth Taft was to be the Republican candidate, and with Locher's reputation as poor as it was, Stokes would almost surely win in a three-way race. But what Washington wanted was a famous Negro *Democrat,* not a famous Negro independent, and wouldn't Carl please run in the Democratic primary this time? Stokes was more interested in his own future than in LBJ's, and he knew that a direct confrontation with Locher in the primary would still be risky, despite the low public esteem to which Locher had sunk. Stokes had learned to appreciate the power of bigotry and fear. The Hough riots were still too vivid in Cleveland's memory, and the black-power people and the white backlashers were keeping the whole city jittery with veiled threats and counterthreats and dark mutterings of impending trouble. What help could he expect from Washington if he ran in the Democratic primary? Certainly no direct help, but at least he could be assured that Locher would not get any comfort from the shores of the Potomac. Stokes delayed his decision but began to circulate two sets of nominating petitions—one as an independent and one for the Democratic primary.

Stokes began to receive invitations to White House functions. Nothing was said there, of course, about the mayoral race in Cleveland, but the message was clear nonetheless: Democrats get invitations to dine at the White House; independents don't.

In July 1967, to the surprise of most Cleveland political observers but to the absolute delight of Washington, Carl Stokes filed his nominating petitions to run, not as an independent, but in the Democratic primary, against Ralph Locher on October 3, 1967.

10. DON'T VOTE FOR A NEGRO

PERHAPS the most surprised person in Cleveland was Frank Celeste, a sixty-year-old lawyer and businessman who had staked his own political future on his confidence that Stokes would run as an independent. Celeste had been a successful mayor of Lakewood, one of Cleveland's bedroom suburbs. Since his retirement from that post, he had been active as a real-estate developer and practicing attorney, well regarded in the Cleveland business community and in Democratic circles. He had been notably unsuccessful in his one try for public office since his days as mayor, when he ran in the Democratic primary for state attorney-general and was decisively defeated.

Encouraged by the business community's complete disillusionment with Ralph Locher, Celeste had floated trial balloons all over the city and none had been punctured too badly. Though the newspapers had not promised him their endorsements, it was clear they would no longer endorse Ralph Locher. With someone else respectable in the Democratic primary, someone like himself, for instance, the papers would almost have to support him. And then he would surely have to be considered the favorite in the expected three-man general election with himself, the Democrat; Seth Taft, the Republican; and Carl Stokes, the independent.

And so, Frank Celeste had become the first announced candidate for the Democratic primary. Stokes had already decided to take the risk and run against Ralph Locher, without any other candidates, but Celeste's entry into the race was welcome news, since he would surely draw off some Locher votes.

Locher, a proud, defiant man, who refused to leave office under fire, charged throughout the primary campaign that Celeste had entered the race merely to help Stokes, or, as a variation on this theme, to help Seth Taft. But there is no evidence that Frank Celeste was motivated by anything other than a sincere, if misguided, belief that at the time he announced his candidacy, the cards seemed stacked for him to win. Later, when the cards began to fall in the wrong direction, it was too late to do anything but stay and play out the game.

The coalition between city hall and the Democratic party, formed for the self-protection of both against Carl Stokes in 1965, stood firmer than ever in 1967, since they now had more to fear, and Chairman Albert Porter, Mayor Ralph Locher, and Law Director Bronis Klementowicz clung tightly to each other.

It is always difficult to fight the man in power in a party primary, and the mayor and the county chairman controlled virtually all the patronage of the county. Most of the five hundred members of the county Democratic executive committee are public employees and so endorsements, which theoretically are decided upon democratically by the members of the committee, are really decided on by the chairman and rubber-stamped by the committee. The disaffection with Locher, however, ran so deep that some committee members began to insist that the chairman open the meeting to nominations for Stokes and Celeste, instead of opening and closing with an endorsement of Locher. Knowing that on a standing vote not more than a handful out of an expected attendance of three hundred at the meeting would dare vote against the party, Porter agreed to an open meeting. He also yielded to press and television pressure and agreed to allow coverage of the meeting.

That was the first of many mistakes Albert Porter was to make throughout a campaign that he now wishes he could forget. Though Locher won the endorsement,

Stokes won the headlines and the television coverage because he was there in person while Locher and Celeste were not. His supporters urged the party to lead the way for the country by showing the political maturity to nominate Carl B. Stokes, whom they all knew to be the best man in any case. All this was dutifully reported in the press the following day, as was Porter's refusal to permit the secret ballot called for by the Stokes people. What was perhaps most significant about the meeting was that its most influential members, the elected county officials, the big money contributors, the judges, the legislators, were conspicuously absent. They dared not openly oppose the chairman, but Stokes was beginning more and more to look like a winner to them, and they didn't want to oppose him, either.

When the standing vote was called for, only seventeen stood for Stokes. But many did not stand at all, and there were only one hundred votes for Locher. It is quite possible that had the absent members been present and willing to put up a fight for Stokes (they all insisted immediately after the primary that they had been for him all along), there would have been a runaway meeting that would have expressed their real choice and resulted in Stokes's endorsement.

By August 1, Stokes already had in operation a highly efficient campaign organization. Office space with room enough to accommodate several hundred campaign workers was obtained in a downtown Cleveland building with the un-Democratic name of the Rockefeller Building. A full-time professional public-relations staff was engaged and began to run full-page ads with such eye-catching messages as "Don't Vote for a Negro—Vote for a Man." Branch offices were established throughout the city; there were the usual mimeograph machines grinding out the thousands of letters, bumper stickers, buttons, and all the paraphernalia of a high-powered political campaign.

Time magazine called the Stokes organization "one of the slickest campaign teams ever to operate in Cleveland." Certainly much of its success could be attributed to its director, Dr. Kenneth Clement, who, as Carl's long-time friend, had taken a leave of absence from his medical practice to manage the campaign full time, because he believed that Cleveland was sicker than any of his patients. Clement, a former president of the National Medical Association, sort of the Negro counterpart of the American Medical Association, is a man who moves easily and confidently back and forth from the Negro to the white world, and his bedside manner, his complete calm, and his superb administrative skills kept the organization functioning. The Stokes headquarters soon came to be known as the place where the action was, and journalists from every part of the country began stopping in to see about this man Stokes who was threatening to put Cleveland back on the map.

The Celeste campaign had never got as high as his trial balloons, which had fallen to earth he knew not where, and at Celeste headquarters, just a few doors up the street from the Rockefeller Building, only Frank's hearty laugh from time to time interrupted the morgue-like silence of the place.

Nothing seemed to be going on at Democratic party headquarters, and, as it turned out, the masterminds of Locher's campaign, aside from organizing the usual ward meetings in the nationality neighborhoods, were spending most of their time turning out a series of dirty little news letters that would prove to be perhaps the biggest mistake of Bert Porter's political life.

With the campaign now getting national attention, contributions, solicited and unsolicited, began to come in from all over the country. Stokes attended fund-raising meetings held for him in Washington and New York; but he did not return, as Locher charged during the campaign, with "wagonloads of gold." There was, however, enough money for a professional campaign. His total campaign budget in 1965 was only $45,000. In the 1967 campaign, he was to spend five times as much.

But regardless of the funds, regardless of the workers, regardless of the material, regardless of the organization, a political campaign can be only as good as its candidate. Carl B. Stokes set out to deliver his message to Cleveland.

11. THE BELIEVER

FOR many years Clevelanders had been immune to the criticisms hurled at their city by newspapers and magazines throughout the country, but by 1967 the evidence was too plain to be ignored. A once vital city, Cleveland was now filled with fear and frustration, doubt and disillusionment, blight and bitterness.

Carl Stokes sensed the malaise that held the people rooted in despair, and determined to renew their faith. He was convinced that for too many years the city had been governed by people who believed in its past but not in its future, and said as much in one of his early campaign speeches:

> The coming election will be a turning-point in the civic, cultural, and economic life of Cleveland. We have a definite choice—continued stagnation and dismal decay of both our physical surroundings and our spirits, or an energetic and enthusiastic forward thrust. I believe in Cleveland. I believe that the people of Cleveland can show the world that they are capable of solving the pressing problem of a great city—that they can show the world that American cities and American civilization can survive and flourish, to the personal benefit of every man, woman, and child in this community. This is the great challenge of the last third of the twentieth century. How we meet the challenge will determine the fate and future of our families, our city, and our country.

This was heady stuff for a city whose mayors usually campaigned for office on a program of honesty and clean habits at city hall, and law and order in the streets. The people desperately wanted a leader. Could this be he? A black Moses come to lead the city of Cleveland out of the wilderness?

Stokes's "I believe in Cleveland" speech has the same sort of messianic appeal as did Martin Luther King's "I Have a Dream" speech of the 1963 Washington civil-rights march. But, while it is true that King was in Cleveland off and on during the summer of 1967 in connection with voter-registration drives; and while the two men encountered each other from time to time at various civil-rights meetings throughout the country and conferred on several occasions in Cleveland, there is no evidence that Stokes received any advice or assistance from King on speech-writing, or that King played a significant part in the campaign at all, though his presence in Cleveland certainly was of great help to Stokes and other responsible Negro leaders in keeping the energy of various black nationalist groups channeled in constructive directions. The threat of violence, of course, was a constant source of worry to Stokes throughout the campaign, and a special task force was available at all times to deal with sensitive situations that arose from time to time. Actually, the only violence that did occur during the entire campaign was that directed by whites against Stokes's west-side campaign headquarters. On four separate occasions during August and September, bricks were hurled through the plate-glass window. The Stokes workers, who had been told to avoid violence at all costs, simply replaced the glass each time—and moved their chairs a little farther from the window. After the fourth incident, however, a young white worker lost his cool and took off down the street after the four white toughs who had thrown the bricks. They turned on him at the corner and beat him severely before he could be rescued. It required all the tact and persuasiveness of the special task force to dissuade some east-side militants from carrying out a reprisal raid.

But if King's presence in Cleveland was comforting to some, it was alarming to others, notably Albert Porter, who began distributing a so-called "News letter from Cuyahoga County Democratic Executive Committee," warning Cleveland's white Democratic voters to "keep Martin Luther King out of city hall." One of these asked:

> Will Dr. Martin Luther King actually be the mayor of Cleveland if Carl Stokes is elected Tuesday? This would give the noted racist control of his first city in the United States. He is in Cleveland now blackmailing reputable business people, telling them who should be promoted, and to place money in Negro banks and advertising in Negro newspapers.

Still another:

> Do you want Dr. Martin Luther King and his disciples running your lives? Do you want earned promotions and job advancements to be canceled and placed on a race basis? Do you want to be told to place your money in a Negro bank? Do you want to be told to sell your home and used car through a Negro newspaper? This is what the King-Stokes combine stands for.

The fact that they all bore the signature of Albert Porter was as disturbing as the contents themselves. For, while Porter might never win any liberal-of-the-year award, he had always seemed like a decent enough man who ran his county engineer's office efficiently and whose one beef seemed to be those suburbanites who were resisting his projected expressways through their parks and tree-lined streets. Some of the lucky readers on the newsletter mailing list thought they detected the heavy hand of Bronis Klementowicz at work: it was he who was credited with having inspired his boss, Ralph Locher, to call King an extremist when King had come to Cleveland in the aftermath of the Hough riots to try to help heal wounds. The newspapers editorialized against them, members of the Democratic executive committee protested, and Clevelanders suddenly stopped feeling superior to Jackson, Mississippi.

Porter loudly denied having written the letters, and even claimed that sometimes they went out before he had a chance to see them; nevertheless, he accepted full responsibility for them. Stokes was willing to take him at his word and lay that responsibility on him, and one of the first things he did after winning the primary was to call for Porter's resignation as Democratic county chairman.

This dismayed almost everyone—the faithful Stokes supporters and those who now wanted to become faithful Stokes supporters. After all, there was still a tough election against Seth Taft to be won, and unity, not a bitter intra-party fight, was what was needed most. Why not declare a temporary truce with Porter, they urged; after all, there was time enough to remove him after the general election. But Stokes, not one to underestimate the value of political alliances or to dismiss lightly the fine political art of compromise, was willing to unify with everyone *but* Bert Porter. There was no place in the great city he envisioned for Cleveland for a party chairman who exacerbated race relations when the urgent need was for racial harmony.

Carl Stokes carried his "I believe in Cleveland" message to every white neighborhood in the city. He spent much less time campaigning in the Negro east-side wards, and would pass up a two-hundred-voter meeting there to talk with a ten-people house party on the west side. Though the regular Democratic meetings were closed to him, he now had a rapidly growing base of white Cleveland supporters who were able to provide forums for him, where he would explain in detail how he would implement his belief in Cleveland in urban renewal, in police work, in education, in community relations. Sometimes he would talk to these white voters about whispering campaigns:

"I want to get the Negro question out of the way," he would say. "Then we can talk about the issues. I'm telling the people my election would not mean a Negro takeover. It would not mean the establishment of a Negro cabinet."

"Even as Senator Lausche happened to come from the Slovene community, and Judge Celebrezze from the Italian community, my election would mean the mayor just happened to come from the Negro group."

"In 1965 when I ran, they whispered all over the west side and the south side that I was a Negro. They don't have to whisper today. I am a Negro. I am proud of it. I intend to remain one."

The white folks ate it up. The more white voters he saw and talked to, the more white voters he won. Carl Stokes believed in Cleveland, and they were beginning to believe in him.

12. THE LAWYER

SEVERAL legal matters that Carl Stokes had been involved in in 1967 cast their reflection in the election. Now that he had become a public figure, almost all his actions, public or private, were searched for political motivations.

Every Democrat who aspires to high public office in Ohio sooner or later encounters the powerful and somewhat mysterious figure of Cyrus Eaton. Eaton, now in his eighties, was a poor boy from Nova Scotia who came to Cleveland and made good and made good and made good. A tall, strong, handsome, silver-haired man, he would be perfectly cast as the spirit of rugged individualism and free enterprise. But he has some strange habits for a tycoon.

For one thing, this rugged capitalist probably enjoys a better personal relationship with the ruling clique in the Soviet Union than anybody in the State Department. For another thing, he could almost be called a peacenik, and, strangest of all for a Wall Street buccaneer, he likes eggheads. From time to time he makes his estate in Nova Scotia available for think sessions of intellectuals. These meetings have come to be known as the Pugwash Conferences, named for the area in which he was born and which he now owns. Cyrus Eaton has made and lost several fortunes in a long career of battling the toughest kids in the business establishment, from the railroads to the utilities, to the steel mills, and, finally, to the Cleveland Trust Company. And that is where Carl Stokes comes in.

Eaton is one of the largest individual shareholders of the Company, but he has no effective voice in the management. He has long claimed that the bank's management was illegally perpetuating itself in office by accumulating large blocks of Cleveland Trust stock in its trust portfolios, which it then voted in favor of itself. In early 1967 a small shareholder of the Company sued the bank to enjoin this practice of voting its trust shares, claiming that it violated Ohio's banking laws. The lawyer for the plaintiff was Carl B. Stokes, and it was immediately charged that Stokes had commenced the litigation on behalf of Cyrus Eaton. (The litigation is still pending.

but Stokes, now occupied with other matters, no longer represents the plaintiff.)

It was surely more than coincidental that Cyrus Eaton's high-powered public-relations man later turned up as PR man for the Stokes campaign, and it was charged (and undenied) that it was Eaton who picked up the tab. Nor was speculation about a Stokes-Eaton alliance diminished by the fact that Eaton's wife was an active volunteer worker at Stokes headquarters. Mrs. Eaton, incidentally, is the daughter of a former, and ex-wife of a present, partner in Jones, Day, Cockley, and Reavis, which, of course, is Seth Taft's law firm and which represents the Cleveland Trust Company. Politics in Cleveland sometimes seems to be wound in an ever-narrowing circle.

And so to those who wouldn't believe that Martin Luther King would be running city hall, the Locher people were able to say that, well, then, Cyrus Eaton would.

Still more fuel was added to the Eaton fire by Stokes. Fifty years ago the city of Cleveland had absorbed a neighboring city that provided its residents with electric power from a municipally owned power plant. Cleveland acquired the plant along with its small neighbor, and has continued to furnish city-owned power to that area of the city—comprising about one fifth of the area and population of Cleveland. The rates charged by the municipal light plant were somewhat lower than those charged by the Cleveland Electric Illuminating Company (which had promoted Cleveland's slogan, "The Best Location in the Nation"), a powerful utility, one of whose large share-

holders was Cyrus Eaton. Stokes argued that the municipal plant should be sold to the illuminating company,
thereby providing badly needed funds in the amount of
$60 million and perhaps as much as $80 million, and
that, furthermore, it was unfair to the majority of the
people of Cleveland for the city to subsidize cheaper
power to a small section. Opponents of the sale argued
that the ownership of the plant by the city had the salu-
tary effect of establishing a lower level for electric-power
rates.

It is likely that Carl's position cost him some votes,
particularly by those who thought he was taking his stand
as a favor to Eaton. In fact, however, he had raised the
same issue in 1965 at a time when he had no known connection with Eaton. It seemed to him that the city of
Cleveland, with more than enough governmental problems weighing it down, could do without the added burden of the electric-power business. Naturally the 175,000
Clevelanders whose light bills were 10 per cent cheaper
because they used municipal power disagreed. Stokes
might have lost even more votes had he not later modified
his position.

Another legal case that Carl handled in 1967 and that
had a significant bearing on his political career was that
of Stokes versus the Cleveland Browns. In a city whose
residents in recent years had little to be proud of, two
local institutions of proven excellence have been tightly
embraced with fierce and jealous love—the Cleveland
Symphony Orchestra and the Cleveland Browns football
team.

In July 1967, as the Cleveland Browns prepared to depart for their summer training camp, Carl Stokes publicly announced, as the lawyer for five of the Browns' Negro players, that his clients would report to camp only when certain contract matters and questions about conditions of employment were resolved with the Browns' management, and not before. One of the five players was Leroy Kelly, who had become the Browns' biggest hero after the retirement of Jimmy Brown. If Stokes had handled this particular matter in such a way as to exploit the news value of anything connected with the Cleveland Browns, he got more news than he had bargained for, and most of it bad. The merits of the controversy between the five players and the Browns' management were quickly submerged in the cries of anguish and outrage of Cleveland's football fans, who probably outnumbered Cleveland's voters. (The Browns for years have been filling Municipal Stadium on Sunday afternoons with more than eighty thousand people—about the same number of people who voted for Stokes in the 1965 mayoral race.) Both the press and the public reacted as though Carl Stokes was proposing that the Browns play the Green Bay Packers with just six players instead of eleven. (As it turned out, the Browns couldn't have done much worse against Green Bay in 1967 with six players. Final score: Packers 52, Browns 7.)

As a matter of fact, the five players had raised some legitimate questions about the relationship of professional athletes to their "owners," and a challenging and interesting legal problem was hidden in the outcry. It would have been a good case for any other lawyer; for Carl Stokes it was a disaster, proving to be one of the few serious miscalculations he has made in gauging public reaction to his actions.

He later tried to salvage what he could from the wreck by saying that his first duty as a lawyer was to his clients and that he knew that his representation of the players held political dangers for him. This seems improbable, however, since for years he had been keenly aware of the political possibilities of any action he took. More likely he simply misjudged the reaction and blew the play.

He should have known better. His relationship with several of the Browns' players had gone back some years, and he had been especially close to the greatest Brown of them all. Carl had helped Jim Brown set up the Negro Industrial and Economic Union, an organization designed to provide financial and technical assistance to Negro-owned and -operated businesses. (The union in the spring of 1968 was given a $500,000 grant by the Ford Foundation. For the most part disdaining ideology, as does Carl Stokes, the union's pragmatic approach to ghetto problems coincides with Stokes's political approach, namely: "The Negro is asked to pull himself up by his bootstraps. But he has no boots." The union is designed to provide some boots.) In 1967 Brown was serving as national chairman, and Stokes as general counsel, of the union. Jim had already retired from football and was in Hollywood fighting Indians and Nazis when the directors of the union decided to use his fame as a fund-raising device. Accordingly, a Jim Brown appreciation night was planned, with a program of entertainment, at the Cleveland Arena. Since many of the country's most famous professional athletes would be in town for the event, the union's directors decided to exploit their presence by inviting one hundred of the Browns' more affluent fans to a hundred-dollar-a-plate dinner at which they could meet, talk, and dine with the likes of Muhammad Ali, *ne* Cassius Clay, Jim Brown, Bobby Mitchell, Bill Russell, Gale Sayers, Bob Hayes, Tim Brown, Mudcat Grant, and assorted split ends and defensive backs.

The dinner was a great success, with Carl Stokes presiding at the table of honor, flanked by Jim Brown and Muhammad Ali. It was plain that this room full of the country's most famous Negro athletes admired Stokes as much as the pop-eyed football fans were admiring *them*. After all, lots of guys can run the hundred in 9.6, but few had ever made it in the white man's world the way Carl Stokes was sure to do. Professional athletes form a special kind of aristocracy in this country, and it was a rare sight to see these black knights of the gridiron, the diamond, the court, and the ring stand in awe of someone who had a weak left hook, couldn't hit a curve ball or sink a basket, and couldn't tell the difference between a Z-out and a flare.

Carl Stokes has maintained a good relationship with all the members of this elite, but he has been especially close to Jim Brown and, to a lesser extent, Muhammad Ali.

Stokes, who worries a great deal about black nationalism and who has, at best, managed only an uneasy truce with the nationalists of his own city, seems genuinely to like Muhammad Ali, who, in fact, when his public guard is down, is an easy man to like. Though Stokes respects his desire not to be called Cassius Clay, he is too nervous about nationalism to call him Muhammad Ali, and so calls him Champ, a name to which his friend is glad to answer.

There are those who believe it was Brown, who had his own problems with the management of the Cleveland Browns, who was responsible for Stokes's involvement with the five recalcitrant players, whose strike got them nothing more than a five-yard penalty for delay of game.

Stokes knew before the vote was in that the fight had been lost, and in the end a relieved Browns management tried to get him off the hook with Cleveland's football fans by announcing that his skillful mediation had resolved the problem and that everyone was happy. But everyone wasn't. Two of the striking players were traded, and Leroy Kelly, though he played through the season and led the league in rushing, refused to sign a new contract. Some of the more unforgiving fans who had attended the dinner and had been contributors to the Stokes campaign in 1965 refused to contribute in 1967 out of resentment for what they thought Stokes had done to their beloved Browns.

But the Browns' loss was Kelly's gain. At the end of the season, having become a free agent, he was able to negotiate a new four-year $320,000 contract with the Browns' management—a display of economic power equal to Stokes's demonstration of political power.

This was not the first time that Carl Stokes had clashed with the Browns' management. In the fall of 1965 a Hollywood movie company was in Cleveland to shoot scenes of the Browns and Municipal Stadium which were to appear in a film called *The Fortune Cookie*. In order to attract a crowd necessary for background shots, the company had arranged with the Browns' management to promote a free show at the stadium, with prizes for all who were willing to come and stay long enough for the necessary scenes to be shot. Why these scenes could not have been shot on a day when a game was being played is unclear, but the date finally selected was November 2, 1965, election day—the day on which the voters of Cleveland were to choose their next mayor among Locher, Stokes, Perk, and McAllister. The sensitive political antenna of Carl Stokes immediately sensed a plot. Those most likely to be attracted to the stadium on a Tuesday by offers of entertainment and prizes would be unemployed people, and most of the unemployed people in Cleveland were Negroes. (Cleveland's unemployment rate has ranged between 3 and 4 per cent in recent years. The unemployment rate among Cleveland's Negroes has been closer to 15 per cent—the most extreme disparity in the nation. Another first for Cleveland.) Since the stadium is a city-owned facility, Stokes claimed that the choice of election day for the show was a plot to keep as many Negroes as possible away from the polls. He immediately fired off telegrams to the movie producer, to city hall, and to the management of the Cleveland Browns, stating his objections and demanding a change of date.

The Browns and city hall ignored the telegrams, but movie producers are notoriously sensitive to political controversy, and the producer began to complain about the Browns' involving Hollywood in Cleveland politics. Art Modell, president and majority owner of the Browns, was not amused. He had chosen the date himself, to fit the football team's schedule, and city hall had not even been consulted. He insisted to Stokes that no other date was possible, but offered to include reminders to vote in the advertisements and announcements of the stadium program. The newspapers were beginning to take note of the controversy, and Stokes was clearly coming out second best to the Browns. He beat a hasty retreat, and the movie scenes were shot on schedule on election day, 1965. So, two years later, when Stokes turned up offside again, Modell hit hard and fast in the newspapers and the game was soon over. But all's well that ends well. The Browns, after a slow start, had a winning season, and Carl B. Stokes is the mayor of Cleveland.

Still, there is a lesson here for all Cleveland politicians. Do what you will with city hall, but don't mess around with the Browns.

Jim Brown had been determined to help Carl Stokes no matter how much he hurt him in the process. While Stokes and Modell were feverishly trying to resolve the players' dispute without too much loss of face to anyone, Brown issued a statement in Los Angeles supporting the position that had originally been taken by Stokes and the players. But Cleveland's fans, who did not have the same love for Jim Brown, film star, that they had had for Jim

Brown, football star, tended to side even more strongly with Art Modell, and Brown had nothing more to say in public about the controversy.

His name was to figure once more, however—this time in connection with the actual campaign. He and Sammy Davis, Jr., planned a Carl Stokes fund-raising reception in Hollywood at which the candidate himself would appear. But Stokes was already becoming sensitive to all the charges of outside money and influence, and he didn't want to be accused of bringing in "wagonloads of gold" from the West Coast, as well as from New York and Washington. So the party was held as scheduled—but without the candidate—and, while some money was raised, it was certainly no wagonload.

Still another legal transaction in which Stokes took part in 1967 was to become an issue in the primary campaign. Stokes, at every opportunity, had reminded Clevelanders that of the three men who were trying to retire Ralph Locher to private life, only he, Stokes, was a bona fide, native-born and -bred Clevelander. Seth Taft, of course, was a Cincinnatian who had come to Cleveland only in 1947 and who, for the most part, had lived in a home appropriate for a Taft in the exclusive residential suburb called Pepper Pike—fifteen miles and two cities removed from Cleveland. He had, of course, rented a house within the Cleveland city limits just before announcing his candidacy, but the Pepper Pike home never lost its lived-in look.

Frank Celeste, though closer to Cleveland than Taft, could be packed in the same carpetbag, since he had spent many years in Lakewood, a suburban city adjoining Cleveland's west-side area, and in fact had served as the first Democratic mayor that Republican community had had in a quarter of a century.

Imagine Ralph Locher's delight, then, to hear that Carl Stokes had apparently purchased a home in Shaker Heights just three weeks before the Primary. If true, Locher could be considered the only *real* Clevelander in the race (although he himself had been born in Rumania), and it did appear to be true, or at least half-true. The Democratic news letter circulated photostatic copies of a deed from the county recorder's office showing the transfer on September 21 of a $30,000 Shaker Heights home to Carl B. Stokes and Louise Stokes.

"Do we want to back a candidate who may pick up his marbles and flee to the suburbs when he doesn't win?" the news-letter gleefully asked.

"After he is defeated on October 3, does he plan to move to the plush suburb to be near many members of his campaign committee who live outside Cleveland?

"Records in the county recorder's office show real-estate file number 113537 as the house at 3718 Lindholm Road that Stokes purchased—strange indication of his faith in Cleveland . . .

"Mayor Ralph S. Locher has Clevelanders on his campaign committee . . .

"He lives in Cleveland, intends to stay in Cleveland . . .

"The Lindholm Road home is also a short drive down Route 8 from the pedigreed cattle and Troika ranch of multi-millionaire financier Cyrus Eaton, whose wife,

Anne, visited Stokes's headquarters and gave a hand Thursday.

"Let's get out the vote for Mayor Locher on October 3 . . . a man who has the interest of Cleveland home owners at heart."

The breathless news-letter readers wondered if Stokes had made another mistake. But it turned out to be not a boner but a booby trap. There is a well-known football play that Carl might have learned from his friends and clients on the Cleveland Browns called the "mousetrap." In this fiendish maneuver, a lineman on the offensive team permits an opponent to come charging unmolested through the line intent upon grabbing an armful of glory in the defenseless form of the quarterback or whichever back happens to have custody of the ball at the moment. But then the trap is sprung and a blocker, who has been lurking nearby, cuts the stampeding lineman down in the prime of life.

Carl Stokes now sprang his trap. The Louise Stokes whose name had appeared as one of the grantees in the Shaker deed was Carl's mother. The house had been purchased for her, for her own use, and Carl's name had appeared on the deed only because it was impossible for a woman of Mrs. Stokes's age, without substantial assets or earnings, to obtain mortgage financing. Well, Carl said, ever so many times, if it was a political risk for him to help his seventy-five-year-old widowed mother buy a modest home in the suburbs, the very suburbs in which she had spent so many years as a domestic servant, that was a risk he would have to take. No political considerations were going to interfere with the comfort and happiness of this wonderful woman who had worked so hard all her life for him and his brother.

A lot of things have gone wrong in Cleveland, Ohio, but motherhood still lives, and everyone was too busy drying tears to suggest that political risk could have been avoided entirely simply by putting the deed in someone else's name—brother Lou's, for example—or by keeping the transaction in escrow for another month.

In what was possibly the last law suit for many years to come in which Stokes would appear, there was no need for speculation as to possible political implications. The connection was clear and direct in the case of Carl B. Stokes, plaintiff, versus Ralph Locher and the Cleveland Board of Control, an action brought in the summer of 1967 in Common Pleas Court of Cuyahoga County.

One of the many things for which the newspapers had lately been attacking Locher had been the alleged secrecy of the Cleveland Board of Control, two members of which were the mayor and his old friend, law director and political adviser, Bronis Klementowicz. The board, which had the authority to award contracts, had been conducting its deliberations in secret session and then going through the motions of a public meeting merely to announce the contract awards. The critics claimed that this violated the public-meeting requirement, since it was impossible to determine on what basis, and upon what considerations, contracts were being awarded. Two disappointed bidders had been successful in getting judicial cancellation of contracts on this ground, but still the secret meetings continued. Carl Stokes, as plaintiff and not as lawyer, brought suit to enjoin the board from exercising its duties in this fashion, and further charged that Klementowicz was perpetuating the secret-meeting device in order to reward city contractors who had been generous in their campaign contributions to the administration.

It was a legitimate lawsuit but one that, had it been brought by someone else, might not have compromised the possibility of a definitive judicial determination, which was badly needed. Stokes, of course, now claims that the matter is moot, since there will be no more secret meetings of the Board of Control.

13. THE LIQUIDATOR

VERY few mayors of major American cities have been the target of as much criticism as Ralph Locher had been during his last two-year term. Civic organizations, ad hoc committees, the newspapers (local and national), magazines, the United States civil-rights commission, urbanologists, and various other observers, critics, and kibitzers had all begun to view Cleveland with alarm, if not horror, and most of them blamed Locher for what they saw. Much of this blame may have been unfair, since urban disease has become a national epidemic, and Cleveland's case was only a little more severe than most. The newspapers finally abandoned him, the *Plain Dealer* endorsing Stokes, and the *Press* endorsing no one but urging a vote for either Stokes or (preferably) Celeste *against* Locher. Since by this time no one in Cleveland expected Celeste to get more than 10 per cent of the votes, this strange editorial stance of the *Press,* a paper that likes to go with a winner, led to a strong suspicion that it was feeling guilty for having encouraged Celeste to enter the race in the first place. It could not risk its prestige on an outright endorsement of a sure loser, but it owed him at least half an endorsement. Less charitable readers of the *Press* speculated that it feared alienating its readers by an outright endorsement of Stokes and so pretended to prefer Celeste. The *Press* courts its cosmo-group readers as ardently as Klementowicz courts cosmo voters, regularly devoting special articles, features, series, and sections to the various nationality groups and neighborhoods of Cleveland.

The *Plain Dealer,* by contrast, had made an early, unambiguous, no-bones-about-it endorsement of Carl Stokes, clearly recognizing that he was by far the best of the three Democratic candidates—unlike the year 1965, when it had also thought him the best candidate but, apparently heeding the cry of timid Cleveland leaders that Cleveland wasn't ready for a Negro mayor, endorsed Ralph Locher, who had as little to be said in his favor then as he did in 1967. More likely, it was the *Plain Dealer* that wasn't ready for a Negro mayor in 1965, being owned by the Forest City Publishing Company, a majority of whose shares was held in trust by the Cleveland Trust Company before the paper was sold to the Newhouse chain in 1966.

The *Press* has likewise always presented a safe institutional point of view, being owned by Scripps Howard, a chain not known for its progressivism.

The *Call and Post,* of course, endorsed Carl Stokes. It always has and probably always will.

In the face of this almost unanimous opposition, almost any elected official anywhere would choose an honorable retirement, but Locher and Klem were not only determined to run, they were sublimely confident that they would win. They had lost everything except the cosmos but they had one big thing going for them—fear of the blacks. They also had the Democratic county executive committee and the labor unions, but about the only thing they had in common was this same fear.

Locher's entire political career had been created out of his image of the nice guy with honesty and integrity. It would be foolhardy to tarnish that image with a campaign based on racial fear—he would leave that part of the campaign to Klem and Bert Porter—but without the race issue he would have nothing to talk about. And then Carl Stokes gave him his theme.

Having once advocated the sale of the municipal light plant on the ground that it was unfair for 80 per cent of the people of Cleveland to subsidize cheap power for the other twenty per cent, Stokes next came up with a real-estate proposal concerning the Shaker Lakes. Around the turn of the century, when the city of Shaker Heights was only a developer's dream, a network of small lakes and wooded parks, now almost completely enclosed within Shaker Heights, was deeded by John D. Rockefeller to the city of Cleveland on the condition that the land be preserved for park purposes. The Van Sweringen brothers, who owned most of the rest of the area that was to become Shaker Heights, persuaded the city of Cleveland to lease this park land to the infant city of Shaker Heights for one dollar a year plus the promise to preserve and maintain the parks. It has been so ever since, and beautiful suburban homes now adorn the shores of Shaker Lakes. It seemed unreasonable to Stokes that Cleveland, a city with hardly a penny in its pocket, should be so generous to Shaker Heights, a city whose per-capita income is among the highest in the country. Why not sell the Shaker Lakes to Shaker Heights, or, if that were impossible under the grant, then at least ask a decent rental for this tremendously valuable property?

The third issue that Stokes had raised and that enabled Locher to raise *his* issue was Stokes's promise that one of his first acts as mayor would be to fire Police Chief Richard Wagner. All the bitterness between the white and black communities of Cleveland had polarized around the stern figure of Chief Wagner, a career cop whose automatic response to any situation was to get tough. The United States civil-rights commission had included in its report a 1959 case which it considered to be an unjustified (and unpunished) killing of a Negro motorist in Cleveland by a white policeman, and tensions between Negroes and the police department, personified by Richard Wagner, had intensified steadily since that date.

In recent years, Wagner had conducted a running feud with a ghetto organization known as J.F.K. House. (The name means Jomo Freedom Kenyatta, not John Fitzgerald Kennedy.) A young Negro militant named Lewis Robinson had effectively organized a group of radical young blacks into a club, a group, a movement, a political party, an army, no one was really quite sure, which had set up headquarters in a slum building they called the J.F.K. House. Robinson, who had earned the respect of his young rebels, was watched closely by Wagner, who claimed that J.F.K. House was simply a training school for making Molotov cocktails and not, as Robinson insisted, an effort to give pride, self-reliance, and identity to his followers.

Wagner gave no freedom to J.F.K. House, and even had the building shut down because of alleged violations of building and sanitary regulations. (A similarly strict application of the law would have closed most of the buildings in the ghetto.) Robinson has been arrested on several occasions and he and his followers (including some whites) have claimed persecution while Wagner claimed revolution. Robinson and J.F.K. House were among the nationalist groups who helped "cool it for Carl" during the campaign, and Robinson was one of those with whom Stokes met regularly during the summer of 1967 to help avert the long, hot summer.

To neutralize as much as possible the adverse reaction

his proposal was certain to arouse in most of the white community, Stokes coupled his announcement to fire Wagner with a promise that his successor would be chosen from among four top officials in the police department, all of whom he named, described, and praised. Each of these police officials was white and each had his own substantial following, both in the police department and in the white community. The Negro community had nothing against any of these men. They would be satisfied with Wagner's head.

Locher joined these three Stokes proposals—sell the light plant, sell Shaker Lakes, and fire Chief Wagner—into an unlikely trinity and fashioned a speech in which he referred to Stokes as "the great liquidator."

Locher would dash from white ward club to white ward club warning them that Stokes was out to liquidate the municipal light plant. Out to liquidate Shaker Lakes. (It is difficult to conceive what vote appeal Locher imagined this issue to have for him. The cards would seem to be stacked on the Stokes side of this argument. After all, he was proposing to get money for Cleveland from Shaker Heights for something Clevelanders do not, in any case, use.)

And then Locher would say that Stokes, not satisfied with liquidating Cleveland's property, also wanted to liquidate Police Chief Richard Wagner, that J. Edgar Hoover of Cleveland, that protector of wives and children, that keeper of law and order in the streets. His audience beginning to be properly horror-stricken, he would then conjure up a nasty vision of the streets of

Cleveland being overrun with hoodlums and racketeers (a sly form of racism subtle enough to preserve his good-guy image).

Finally, reaching his peroration, Locher, looking his most sincere, would state grandly that even though Carl Stokes, the great liquidator, might think Cleveland was for sale, he, Ralph S. Locher, was not.

Stokes's response to this speech was always: "Of course Ralph Locher's not for sale. Who would want to buy him?" (Locher at least has the distinction of having inspired most of the best lines of the campaign. Seth Taft used to say about him: "Ralph Locher says he's running on his record. Well, that's fine with me because *I'm* running on his record too." Though Taft was running unopposed in the Republican primary, he would make a campaign speech from time to time just to keep his legs in shape for the long sprint from Pepper Pike to city hall.)

Cleveland still owns the municipal light plant and the Shaker Lakes and it remains to be seen whether or not Stokes will liquidate them. But it seems clear that he has liquidated Ralph S. Locher.

14. ABRAHAM LINCOLN
SLEPT HERE

A
S OCTOBER 3, primary election day, drew near, Stokes intensified his campaign in the west-side white wards. During the previous six years he had carefully cultivated the friend-ship of every person he met who might be of some polit-ical help to him. He has the knack, invaluable to a politi-cian, of making one feel that he alone is the person Carl Stokes *really* trusts, the person whose opinions and judg-ments he *really* admires, the person who *really* knows Carl Stokes, the man who is indeed his friend. But, aside

from his brother Lou, his campaign manager, Ken Clement, and possibly Jim Brown, it is doubtful that anyone is really close to Carl Stokes. He has been too busy making allies to make friends. With each passing year, he appeared more and more often at parties of white suburbanites, who would later become valuable sources of campaign contributions and campaign workers, each of whom would be assured by the warmth of Carl's gratitude that it was *his* contribution that had put the campaign over the top, or *his* work in the registration drive that had got out the winning votes.

But he is no more cynical about whites than he is about blacks. He is at home in both worlds and seems to believe that it is his mission to bridge the gap between those worlds. He scoffs at black power and he scoffs at white power, for to him political power has no color, and he is un-self-conscious enough to deal easily with race. He has shrewdly judged white fears, and has told white audiences that he is proud to be a Negro. But these sound more like the words of a PR man than like those of Carl Stokes. It is just as likely that he would say, and mean, he is proud to have two arms or two legs. He is a proud man who is a Negro but he is not a proud Negro. His color is a fact of his being—a fact that concerns him only to the extent that it is one more political factor to be measured and weighed on the scales of his ambition.

When he says "I believe in Cleveland" he seems really to believe, and his pride and confidence and self-assurance were reassuring to Clevelanders, white and black, who had grown weary of disillusionment.

He has earned his popularity in the black community in exactly the same manner—with his earnestness and the force of his personality, not automatically because of his color. He had had to earn those votes as he would any votes. "Let me say this to you," he would tell Negro groups, "any Negro who thinks he is going to get Negro votes just because he is a Negro is in for a rude awakening."

He had won their loyalty by appealing directly to them, and in most cases without the co-operation of the Negro councilmen. (In the 1965 campaign only two out of the ten Negroes in council had supported him.) The political views of the black community covered the entire political spectrum, but liberal or conservative, Democrat or Republican, militant or passive, Uncle Tom or defiant rebel—to each he would stress the superiority of political action to violence as the answer to ghetto problems.

He is not a hero to all blacks, and nationalists are suspicious of him as they are of any who deviate from their view of society. He himself is not at all sure that he can solve the problem of incipient violence and revolt in Cleveland's ghetto, but at least he knows whom to talk to and what to say.

He had had considerable help in 1967 in maintaining a state of non-belligerency on the ghetto front. Martin Luther King had lent support with his registration drive and fair-employment campaign. Probably of greater help was the local chapter of the Congress of Racial Equality, which, though relatively small, was feeling prosperous with the grant of $175,000 it had received from the Ford Foundation for political-education activities in Cleveland. CORE's stance, of course, was much more militant than that of Martin Luther King (and of Carl Stokes, for that matter), and so CORE was received with much less suspicion and hostility by the Muslims, by the nationalists, by RAM, by Snick, and by J.F.K. House. There were cries of outrage and anguish from the Locher group when CORE received its grant, and it must indeed have seemed to Ralph Locher that the whole country was conspiring to put him out of office. On October 2 CORE ran a full-page ad in the *Call and Post* telling the Negroes: "If You Don't Vote This Tuesday, Forget It."

CORE's rapport with the black youth leaders undoubtedly helped to cool it in the ghetto, and the *Call and Post* ad, being a message from CORE and not from or for (directly) Carl Stokes, must surely have brought out black voters who would otherwise have stayed at home. And though they may not have particularly liked Carl Stokes, they were not about to vote for Mr. Charley.

Ralph Locher may have had a point when he complained that the CORE ad, if paid for with Ford Foundation money, was an improper use of funds given for registration and voter education and *not* for the support of a candidate. But the votes have already been counted, and Locher will have to take his complaint up with McGeorge Bundy.

All the public-opinion polls taken in the weeks before the primary had been ambiguous, but poll takers like to be decisive, and though they were unable to forecast the winner with any certainty, they unequivocally announced that Frank Celeste would be the loser. The *Press* and the *Plain Dealer,* apparently finding it difficult to believe that Cleveland was *really* ready for a Negro mayor, both predicted victory for Locher by a narrow margin.

Almost the only person willing to publicly predict a victory for Carl Stokes was Carl Stokes. In the final days before the primary, he seemed to grow more relaxed even as the workers at Stokes headquarters grew more nervous.

There had been fear of widespread crossovers by Republican voters attempting to vote a Democratic ballot in the primary in order to "help keep the nigger out of city hall." In Ohio, a registered voter who has not voted in primary elections and is thus classified as an independent, or one with a party designation who at the primary seeks to vote the ballot of the other party, may be challenged at the voting booth. Under the law of Ohio, a voter thus challenged is required to sign an affidavit stating that in the last previous general election in which he voted, he cast his vote for a majority of candidates of the party whose ballot he now seeks to vote. If he is willing to sign the affidavit, he cannot be denied the ballot.

The Stokes staff had recruited and trained an army of 903 poll watchers, one for each of Cleveland's 903 precincts, whose duty it would be to challenge suspected Republican crossovers and witness the vote count. (The absence of voting machines in the primary led to the fear of careless or corrupt vote-counting, since election officials are employees of the County Board of Elections, the members of which are appointed by the party county chairmen.) The Stokes challengers were instructed to make their own count as the election-booth officials made theirs, and to report immediately to Stokes headquarters the totals and the number of the last ballot voted at that polling place (so as to rule out any additional ballots). The efficiency of this witnessing operation was typical of the thoroughness of the Stokes staff, which in just three months had put together campaign machinery better than anything the party organizations had ever been able to manage.

Primary day dawned bright, sunny, and warm, but the climate would neither help nor hurt any of the candidates. At least the weather in Cleveland is non-discriminating, and it was bright, sunny, and warm all day all over the city—in the ghetto, in the cosmo wards, on the west side. There were a rash of early challenges, and many white voters who were designated other than Democrat in the poll book refused to sign affidavits. Crossovers, however, proved to be an insignificant factor. Polling places close at 6:30 P.M. in Cleveland, and half an hour later Stokes witnesses were already beginning to phone in results that were being received over a battery of telephones in an upper floor of the Rockefeller Building and quickly tabulated. Every few moments a current tabulation would be rushed downstairs to the candidate, who was calmly watching the election returns on television in the back-room private office with Ken Clement and several other top-echelon members of his staff. Relaxed, smoking a big cigar (something he does only in private), Stokes seemed unperturbed by the early returns that showed a big lead for Locher. He was, in fact, immediately encouraged, because totals from the Negro wards had yet to be reported, and he seemed to be receiving a larger percentage of white votes than he had calculated necessary to win.

In the outer offices the Stokes supporters were less sanguine. Though they also knew that the Negro wards were usually the last to be counted, their confidence was being shaken by the early-evening inaccuracies and bogus expertise of radio and television commentators who by 8:00 P.M. were beginning to announce that Ralph Locher had apparently been renominated for a fourth term.

Meanwhile, hundreds of Stokes supporters had begun to converge on Stokes headquarters, and when the outer rooms and the lobby of the building were jammed, this band of true believers, black and white, began to spill out into Superior Avenue. There this happy group, sensing victory in spite of the experts' opinions, danced in the street as the Stokes campaign combo played "East Side, West Side" and "Happy Days Are Here Again," election music relevant to any campaign. Cleveland's streets had not seen such a mood for many years. Just one year earlier, for example, sullen, angry, bitter, frightened crowds had filled the streets of Hough. Could a dead city really be brought back to life? Something clearly was happening in Cleveland, Ohio.

The Rockefeller Building, in front of which these electoral rites of fall were being performed by this mixed crowd of white and colored (it appeared to be about fifty-fifty, though nobody counted), was at one time one of Cleveland's grandest office buildings. But, like most of the rest of Cleveland, it had fallen into a sad state of disrepair. Only a few blocks away from the main business section, it was a forgotten, neglected, half-empty building. In 1966, determined to restore the grand old lady to her former glory, a group of young Cleveland real-estate developers acquired it, and offered Stokes free headquarters space, calculating that the attention and publicity aroused by the campaign could do it no harm. Furthermore, there are worse friends for a real-estate developer to have than the mayor.

During the face-lifting of the old girl, the new owners were delighted to discover on the façade a brass inscription that had been covered over and encrusted by years of exposure to the soot and grime and smoke that drifted across the flats from the steel mills visible from the upper floors of the building:

IN THE WEDDELL HOUSE
ON THIS SITE
ABRAHAM LINCOLN SPENT
THE NIGHT OF FEBRUARY 15, 1861

It is tempting to speculate whether Carl Stokes ever pondered that plaque and imagined for a moment a different inscription on that corner in the centuries to come:

FROM HIS OFFICES ON THIS SITE
IN THE ROCKEFELLER BUILDING
CARL B. STOKES WAS ELECTED
MAYOR OF CLEVELAND ON NOVEMBER 7, 1967

Things were much quieter a few blocks away in the Carter Hotel, where Klementowicz sat stony-faced in Locher headquarters examining the same kind of precinct reports that were being handed to Carl Stokes. Klem knew the significance of the relatively large number of Stokes votes in the early white-ward returns, and was not misled by the broadcasters' predictions and vote projections. Indeed, he must have known the outcome from the time he saw the first returns, and refused to make a statement to reporters all evening.

At 9:15 P.M., with predictions of a Locher victory still hot on the wires, Carl Stokes announced to the TV broadcasters, who had converted one room of his headquarters into a makeshift studio, that he had an announcement to make. They knew it was too early for a concession of defeat, but perhaps he knew something they didn't. He certainly did. Before a disbelieving TV audience, he calmly announced that the tabulations being made in his headquarters showed clearly and conclusively that he had won the primary election and that his victory margin would exceed ten thousand votes.

He had been too conservative. The final returns showed 110,552 for Stokes, 92,321 for Locher, and only 8,509 for Celeste.

An analysis of the votes showed that the approximate number of whites voting for Stokes had been 18,000—

or 14 per cent—his margin of victory, and of these, many more had come from the cosmo wards than he had expected.

The impossible had happened. A Negro had defeated a white man head to head in an election contest in a city where whites outnumber Negroes by almost two to one. And it had happened in that most unlikely of places—Cleveland, Ohio.

Frank Celeste came immediately to offer his congratulations, to be followed shortly by Mayor Ralph Locher and his wife. Stokes greeted both Celeste and Locher before the TV cameras and then, amid the bedlam, and with his happy but tearful wife Shirley beside him, he began to make a speech. Not a victory speech—he had made that at 9:15 when the primary had ended for him—but the first in his campaign for November 7:

"My heart is full . . . you have vindicated my faith in democracy."

Before he could say more, however, he was interrupted by Ken Clement, who told him that the Vice-President of the United States was on the phone. Stokes apologized to his wildly cheering supporters in the studio, thanked them for their hard work, and, remembering that he was still on camera, thanked all the people of Cleveland, promised them a vigorous, race-free campaign for the general election, and excused himself to take Hubert Humphrey's call. Washington Democrats had already been waiting a long time for Carl B. Stokes.

Meanwhile, being unable to reach and touch the nominee, the wildly jubilant and emotional Stokes workers congratulated, kissed, and embraced everyone in sight —without regard to race, color, creed, or national origin. It was a scene that only Harry Golden could write.

There were, of course, some sour notes that were sounded. Rumors began to spread that Ralph Locher and Chief Wagner had alerted all policemen for possible riot duty in the ghetto, having expected a Locher victory and a violent reaction. Locher was even said to have notified the National Guard to be prepared for immediate assistance.

The young Negro girl who had continued to perform her duties as switchboard operator and receptionist throughout the pandemonium and confusion was overheard telling one caller who obviously had not voted for Stokes:

"You're damn right I'm a nigger lover because I'm a nigger." She seemed very happy.

Seth Taft and Carl Stokes in a debate at the Cleveland City Club, their fifth public confrontation of the 1967 mayoral campaign.

Don't vote for a Negro.

Vote for a man.

Vote for ability. Vote for character.

Vote for experience and intelligence and dedication.

Vote for an organizer. A man who can and will work with our industrial leaders, our bankers, our merchants, our labor leaders, our welfare people, our neighborhood group leaders, our religious leaders, our lawmakers.

Vote for a planner. A man who understands poverty, Cleveland slums, Cleveland's too quiet downtown, Cleveland's under-used seaport, Cleveland's over-used streets.

Vote for a leader. A man who can attack the problems and solve them. A man who can rally the people of Cleveland behind him.

Vote for a man.

A man who believes. Carl Stokes.

"It's time to believe in Cleveland" — Carl Stokes

One of the ads for Carl Stokes which ran in Cleveland newspapers during the campaign.

Stokes seeking votes in downtown Cleveland.

Wide World

The new mayor of Cleveland with his wife, Shirley, after the uphill
victory on election night.

Stokes wipes tears from his eyes during a memorial service for Dr. Martin Luther King, Jr., in the Old Stone Church in Public Square, Cleveland.

With hostesses at John F. Kennedy High School, site of a Town Hall meeting in May 1968.

The first Negro mayor of a major American city.

15. THE UNIFIER

WHAT Carl Stokes understands better than anything else is the use of power. While newspapers, broadcasters, and the rest of the city of Cleveland were indulging in an orgy of self-satisfaction over having been brave enough, mature enough, wise enough, and unprejudiced enough to nominate a Negro for mayor, the nominee on October 4, the morning after the election, had already planned a big unity rally to be held in the Cleveland Music Hall just one week later. The Democratic party was in shambles, and Stokes needed it put back together again to insure his victory over Seth Taft in November. Having already demanded Bert Porter's resignation as county chairman, and having accused Klementowicz of being the villain in the Locher campaign, Stokes found it easy to thank Locher warmly for his congratulations and to say at his headquarters on primary night: "For that action, for coming down here, walking through this mob, in my book Ralph Locher is the biggest man in town."

But that had been last night and this was this morning. Carl B. Stokes was now the biggest man in town, and it was necessary to make that clear immediately to any nervous Democrats who might be tempted to stay away with Klem and Porter.

Telegrams went out to all the leading Democrats of Cleveland inviting them to appear as guests of honor at the meeting on October 12. Senator Stephen Young, remembering Stokes had *not* joined the John Glenn campaign against him, replied that he would be delighted to attend and speak for his friend and fellow Democrat, Carl Stokes.

Congressman Charles Vanik too remembered that Stokes had *not* run against him in the Twenty-first District in Cleveland. He also reflected that if Carl Stokes, now the most popular Democrat in Cleveland, lost the mayoral race he could easily defeat Vanik if he decided to go to Congress. Carl Stokes simply had to be elected mayor. Certainly, replied Vanik, he would do anything he could to help him.

Congressman Michael Feighan, of Cleveland's Twentieth District, perhaps wistfully recalling how his very own flesh and blood, his son William, had once defeated the mighty Carl Stokes in a race for the state legislature, could not afford to say no, his district now encompassing a large number of Negro voters.

Also in Washington, former Ohio Governor Michael V. DiSalle, now a practicing lawyer, would be a good man to have on the platform even though he had never been a Clevelander. DiSalle, the only Italian ever to have served as Ohio's governor, is still remembered warmly by most Italians in Ohio (and by most other Ohioans), and, of course, it was in Cleveland's Little Italy section that Stokes expected to have the most difficulty. Surely DiSalle could do worse than to earn the gratitude of Stokes, the man the national administration and the Democratic national committee considered to be the most important Democrat in Ohio (that is, now that *he* was in Washington). DiSalle immediately accepted the invitation.

James V. Stanton, the young president of Cleveland's city council, whose own visions of the mayor's chair were being rapidly obscured by the smoke of Stokes's blast-off, was reminded by several Negro councilmen that he should certainly attend the rally if he expected their support for president of council.

With acceptances coming in at a rapid rate and being immediately announced in the press, on the air, and by word of mouth, uncertain Democrats could no longer dare sit back and wait to see what everyone else would do. Soon judges, legislators, county officials, councilmen, ward leaders, almost everyone who had been invited and some who had not, were announcing their complete support of, and unity with, Carl Stokes.

Labor, too, was unified. The Cleveland council of the AFL-CIO had endorsed Locher in the primary—not because labor loved Locher but because, undistinguished for its record in civil rights, it had not been ready for a Negro mayor. The AFL-CIO endorsement had been relatively unimportant in the primary, and would probably be an insignificant factor in the general election, since Cleveland labor unions have never been particularly effective in local elections. It is only in state or national elections, where there is an issue or a candidate to frighten them into a frenzy of self-protective political activity, that they are able to exercise an influence commensurate with their numbers.

In Seth Taft, labor thought it had such a candidate; and since it is inconceivable that labor in Ohio could ever endorse a Taft, or even stand by and permit him to run without their opposition, the AFL-CIO was perfectly happy to be unified with Carl Stokes. It is likely that labor in Ohio fears Tafts more than it fears Negroes.

Seth Taft, as a matter of fact, has always taken a more progressive position in public matters than did his Uncle Robert or his cousin, Robert, Jr. There have been many AFL-CIO-endorsed candidates in Ohio who were far to the right of Seth Taft on labor and all other issues. But all politicians have crosses which they must bear from time to time. In 1965 Carl Stokes's was his color; in 1967 Seth Taft's was his name.

And so, the labor representatives, representing 200,-000 union members in Cleveland, spoke warmly of Carl Stokes at the big meeting. So did everyone else who was there. Some of the local Italian officeholders were absent but they had a good excuse, since October 12 was Columbus Day—a conflict in scheduling which Stokes's staff, numbering no Italians, overlooked.

But Mike DiSalle was there, and he alone was as good as a *Nina,* a *Pinta,* and a *Santa Maria* full of Italians. DiSalle spoke of the great American drama that was unfolding and that would see the great grandson of a slave defeat the grandson of a President. He compared the Negro's struggle for recognition with his own personal struggle as an immigrant child who could speak no English and therefore not understand that he was being beaten by other boys in the neighborhood simply because he was different. They would love that story on Murray Hill.

Stokes was grateful for DiSalle's great-grandson-of-a-slave reference. It was a phrase he himself would have been embarrassed to use: too melodramatic to be consistent with his political style.

Great grandson of a slave though he may be (though he suspects it would be hard to prove in a court of law), he does not think of himself in those terms, but they fit DiSalle's style, and Carl would later say in speeches: "As my friend Governor DiSalle said, 'This great grandson of a slave . . .'" or, "As my friend Mike DiSalle put it . . ."

Charles Vanik served as master of ceremonies, and

ridiculed the prophets of doom who had warned of racial trouble: "The day after Carl Stokes was nominated, everything went on just as before. The buses ran, the people worked, and the flags flew a little more freely in front of city hall."

Vanik, of course (not to be outdone by DiSalle), talked about his Slovenian background; and speaker after speaker rose to unify with, moralize about, and praise Carl Stokes.

Full-page ads in the newspapers had invited the public to attend the meeting, which had been designated as the Democratic Unity Rally for Carl B. Stokes:

> We've already taken the first step. . . .
>
> By electing Carl Stokes in the primary, we've shown the nation, indeed the world, that Cleveland is today the most mature and politically sophisticated city on the face of the earth. [The Stokes people were not above indulging in a bit of self-congratulation themselves.]
>
> All the important Democratic public officials will be in attendance: the AFL-CIO executive committee and the major Democratic political leaders and labor leaders. Carl Stokes will be the featured speaker.

Then followed a list of the notables who would be present. It was an honor roll of the Cleveland Democratic power structure, and no Democratic party worker could risk being absent. Over two thousand Democratic workers, including precinct committeemen, ward leaders, and county and city employees showed up and enjoyed the never-before-seen spectacle of a Negro politician, stage center in the spotlight, with one hundred unified Democratic judges, commissioners, congressmen, labor leaders, county officials, and party leaders sitting dutifully behind him on the stage.

It was an awesome display of power. There had been widespread predictions of wholesale Democratic defections if Stokes won the primary. There were even those who said it would be another Gary. Gary, Indiana, is in many respects a smaller version of Cleveland, Ohio, with the same kind of nationality-white population, a large Negro population, a steel-mill economy, and, it was widely assumed, the same prejudices.

In June 1967 Richard Hatcher, a Negro Democrat, had won the Democratic primary for mayor and had then waited for the Democratic party of Gary to support him. He is still waiting. The party instead chose to support the Republican candidate, a rank heresy in Democratic Gary but clearly the lesser of two evils back home in Indiana.

Carl Stokes was determined that this would not happen to him, and starting with the widely publicized telephone call from Hubert Humphrey on election night and the telegrams the following morning, the squeeze was on. No one in Cleveland felt the pressure more than Albert Porter. In the two days following the demand for his resignation, he was unavailable for comment to reporters. What strategy he might have been planning during that time is purely academic, because when he emerged from his seclusion most of his party had already left him. Too many important figures had already committed themselves. Porter was locked in not only by the immediate support of Stokes by local party people, but also by the obvious enthusiasm for Stokes of the national administration and the national committee. Bert Porter had nowhere to go. He couldn't even go to the unity party because he hadn't been invited.

Party regulars who were indebted to Porter for past favors urged Stokes to forget Porter and concentrate on Seth Taft. They were afraid that if he pushed Porter too far there would be no graceful way for Porter to offer support and the party would be split. The Stokes people themselves thought Carl's point had been sufficiently made, and that any further dump-Porter moves could await the election. But Carl left town four days after the primary, taking his family away for a short vacation without having withdrawn his resignation demand.

Porter, swallowing hard, finally agreed to talk to a reporter who asked two questions: Would he resign and would he support Stokes? Porter said that he would not resign, and, as for supporting Stokes, the Democratic party had traditionally supported the Democratic nominee and he saw no reason why it would not do so this year.

Few party leaders have ever been subjected to such humiliation and loss of face. But those Stokes supporters who were tempted to sympathize with the county chairman recalled (1) that he had taken the responsibility for a vicious Democratic news-letter; (2) that in 1965 he had refused to permit Stokes to sit on the platform at Democratic party functions on the ground that he was an independent; and (3) that he had locked the party doors to Stokes again in 1967, calling him a racist Republican.

Carl's extreme reaction to what he believed was Porter's racism came as a surprise to those who had considered Stokes a political pro, hardened by years of experience in a tough political arena. The rules of the game, they argued, sometimes required yesterday's enemies to be today's friends. Stokes knew as well as anyone (and probably better) the rules of the game, but racism was no garden-type variety of weed; it threatened to choke the very life of the city.

If it is possible for a Negro to be an idealist in our society, then Carl Stokes is an idealist. He has the old-fashioned rationalist hope that all society's problems, even those of color, will, in the end, be solved by a serious application of wisdom, learning, and goodwill. He has staked all on his belief that bitterness and hatred between the races is not inevitable in this country. If he is wrong—if the nationalists are right, if the bigots are right —then his entire career has been a mistake and he is wasting his time.

Carl Stokes would never have chosen a political career just to become another Negro politician. There are limits beyond which a Negro politician cannot go—no matter how talented. But there are no limits to the career of a man who can be accepted for his abilities as a man. His ambitions were too vast to be limited by color and so he was determined to neutralize color. He would break the color line of politics. Instead of just playing ball in the Negro wards, he would enter the big leagues and be elected to office by a predominantly white electorate, convincing them that in their own self-interest, life-long habits of thought and attitudes and ingrained prejudices can be, if not forgotten, at least set aside in order to have the services of a better ball player, a better officeholder.

He was an idealist, but he was neither foolish nor naive enough to believe that his color would be of no consequence in a bid for public office. Nevertheless, he would force his adversaries to contend with him as a politician who happened to be a Negro, and not as a Negro politician.

He was not representing Negroes, he was representing himself, and he would not allow every campaign in which he engaged to be an indictment or a defense of the Negro race. That would produce only an endless series of shouting matches and not the kind of dialogue that the races needed if they were ever to stop hating and fearing each other. But one has to learn to talk before there can be dialogue, and in the urban jungle that America's cities had become, people had forgotten how to talk. He would teach them to talk again, and on the level of dialogue, but first there were the problems of unemployment, poverty, disease, crime, urban rot and decay to be attacked and conquered. If the American political genius could not cope with America's urban dilemma then the American dream was a lie, and Carl Stokes refused to believe that it was. Surely the same political ingenuity that created the cities could cure them, as violence and repression could only destroy them. Carl had started his adult life by giving up fighting for politics: he did not want to end his life by giving up politics for fighting.

He would bitterly resist and resent, therefore, any attempt to attack his candidacy by focusing on anyone or anything outside himself. Bert Porter had tried to make Martin Luther King the candidate; he had tried to make CORE the issue; he had warned against filling city hall with the black race. Carl Stokes was not Martin Luther King; he was not CORE; and he was not the black race.

Under extreme pressure from most of the Democrats in town, the Stokes people, who wanted to win only an election, not a crusade, extended an invitation to Porter to sit on the platform but not to speak. Upon his return to Cleveland, Stokes agreed to honor the truce that his staff had arranged, though he made no public statement and refused to withdraw his demand for Porter's resignation. Stokes even allowed himself to be photographed on the platform with Porter, exchanging what appears to be a hearty handshake and a friendly smile. But the famous Stokes smile is missing only in photographs of solemn occasions, which the unity meeting clearly was not supposed to be.

Far from signaling the end of the fight, the clasp of hands almost surely was the traditional handshake before the championship bout begins. Cleveland has a street called Short Vincent Street where Midwest versions of Damon Runyon characters book bets on election as well as race results. Cleveland mayoral candidates always include a very small plank in their campaign platform for "running the bookies off Short Vincent," but of course no mayor ever does that. It now appears that urban renewal will do what the mayors could not: Short Vincent is scheduled to disappear in a downtown development project. Now, however, the odds on Short Vincent are two to one that if Porter refuses to resign and fights for his job he will keep it, because the party-election machinery is so cumbersome and so structured in favor of those who, at the moment, control it, that it is harder to oust a county chairman than it is to remove a mayor. But at least Porter's power can be neutralized by Stokes simply by cutting off city-hall patronage, and by replacing him as Washington's man in Cleveland—and there is no doubt that from Washington's view of Cleveland, Stokes is now the fairest of them all.

16. SZABADSAG

THOUGH there were no off-key notes at Cleveland Music Hall on October 12, two members of the orchestra who could have been playing beautiful Hungarian rhapsodies on first violins failed to appear. Senator Frank Lausche (who is not Hungarian but Slovenian) and Ralph Locher (who is not Hungarian but Rumanian), old friends and political colleagues, had both been invited to the concert but pleaded other engagements. City hall is just across the street from Music Hall, but no one asked Locher why he couldn't just walk over and say hello. Everyone knew why. Locher, as he has usually done in his political career, was waiting to see what Frank Lausche would do. And Lausche, as he has usually done in *his* political career, was doing nothing. Frank Lausche has been the lone wolf of Ohio politics. He has no ties with the Democratic party, either on a state or local level. Ohio labor for years has been trying to defeat him, and he has no personal political organization of any kind. He would be perfect for a southern Democrat, but he is an anomaly for a northern one. (He is always given near-perfect ratings by Americans for Constitutional Action and similar groups.) Though his golfing skill is less well known than Eisenhower's, he could probably give Ike a stroke per hole.

The other thing that Frank Lausche is good at is getting elected. Except for two years in the mid forties, he has been holding an elective office since the thirties. There has been no Cleveland election, or state-wide election, for twenty years in which the candidate has not courted Lausche's support, though very few have ever received it. The late Senator Robert Taft was one who did, in the last campaign of his life in 1950. The Democratic candidate for the Senate that year was a county courthouse politician named Joseph Ferguson, fondly remembered by Ohio Democrats for saying, when asked if he was troubled about the situation on Formosa, that he would take it by three thousand votes.

Ferguson would shock rural Ohio audiences with a most serious charge against Mr. Republican. "Jumping

Joe" (as he was called) would pound the lectern and shout: "My opponent not only went to Yale—he went to Harvard, too."

Taft never denied the charge but he won the election anyway. Ohio Democrats still hold a grudge against Senator Lausche for having openly endorsed the opponent of the Democratic candidate, but that hasn't stopped them from seeking his support in every election. Another of the few who have got it is Ralph Locher. Lausche in 1967 was reluctant to back a mayor who had suffered so much criticism from the newspapers, and he found excuses for being away from Cleveland during the campaign. But, unwilling to abandon his protégé completely, he made an endorsement statement in Washington which Locher made full use of in newspaper ads. Lausche's appeal in Cleveland, however, is with the same voters who were certain to support Locher in any case, and the only beneficiaries of the ads were the newspapers, grateful for more premium-rate political advertisements.

Lausche's support would be much more important to Stokes, of course, than to Locher, because where Lausche was strongest, Stokes was weakest—namely in the so-called cosmo wards of the south and southeast side, tight little islands of eastern and central European immigrants, sons of immigrants, and grandsons of immigrants. These Hungarians, Poles, Czechs, and Croatians, Serbs, Rumanians, and Slovenians clung to a large extent to their own ethnic customs, traditions, foods, and, at least on special occasions, dress. They were thoroughly Americanized in one respect, however: they tended to fear and mistrust Negroes. These ethnic enclaves maintained friendly diplomatic relations with each other and with the white community in general, but travelers through their lands who had black faces were looked upon with suspicion and hostility.

These nationality groups had been the Negroes of the thirties in Cleveland. At that time, colored people constituted only 10 per cent of the population and were easily kept out of sight in the ghetto. Growing up in that ghetto, among that hidden 10 per cent, Carl Stokes had little reason to be concerned about these different people with their strange way of talking and their strange customs. He does remember that sometimes names were called—"nigger" and "hunky," for instance—and though "nigger" has remained the same, "hunky" has become "honky" and to some blacks is a name for all whites.

The full impact of the depression was felt by these nationality groups, who comprised a third of Cleveland's population (as the Negroes now do), and they were the ones at the bottom of the economic and social ladder—unemployed and resentful of the establishment (the Negroes, of course, were even worse off, but they couldn't be seen, having yet to reach the bottom rung). Then along came Franklin Delano Roosevelt, a most unlikely hero who wasn't even related to a Hungarian, Pole, or Czech but who seemed to take their side against those downtown snobs and who promised them economic liberation. FDR won them completely. In Cleveland, Ray T. Miller capitalized on that loyalty by welding the nationality groups of Cleveland into the solid base of

Cleveland's Democratic power. It has been so ever since, except that the cosmopolitan one-third is now matched by the Negro one-third, throwing the balance of power to a less committed one-third, which is the only reason that someone with the unlikely name of Taft could ever dream of running for mayor of Cleveland.

Cleveland's establishment has often exercised its power from the privileged sanctuaries of the all-white, mostly WASP Union Club and Athletic Club. Cleveland's cosmos have exercised *their* power through clubs whose names, if not their membership, are more colorful. In every election Clevelanders can expect to hear from, among many others, the Alliance of Poles of America, the Polish Falcons, the Croatian Club, the Cosmopolitan Club of Cleveland, the Hungarian Business and Tradesmen's Club, the Polish Army Veterans of World War II, the Hungarian Freedom Fighters Circle, the Polish Women's Association, the Slovenian National Home, the Ukrainian American Youth Association, and the Union of Poles in America. Though the hearts of their parents had been won by the New Deal policies of FDR, the loyalty of the present generation had been captured by the middle-European charm of Frank Lausche, who had been the first one of their boys to make it big in Cleveland politics. They didn't seem to care, if they noticed, that Frank Lausche's political views are about as far removed from FDR's as are Barry Goldwater's.

But, though Lausche was the undisputed king of the cosmos, they had formed a reliable base of support for all Democratic candidates in Cleveland. They had been as single-party-minded as old-time southern Democrats, and their votes meant a substantial majority, within the city limits, for any Democratic candidate. With the single exception of county auditor Ralph Perk (who is unique, in any case, since he is a cosmo Republican), no Republican candidate, local, state, or national, had won a majority of the votes in the city of Cleveland for a quarter of a century. Not Robert A. Taft, not John Bricker, not Dewey, not Nixon, not Governor Rhodes, not even Eisenhower.

Frank Lausche could still, in 1967, count those cosmo votes as his, and he would be needing them in 1968 when he would be up for re-election. Lausche studied the primary results in Washington and announced that he would withhold any statement on the general election. He would need time to ponder his dilemma. The Ohio AFL-CIO, he knew, was ready to back any important Democrat brave enough to challenge him in the primary in May. One who was willing to do so was John Gilligan, a Kennedy-type Democrat, who had served one term as Cincinnati's congressman and then been defeated by Robert Taft, Jr., in 1966. Gilligan would be the beneficiary of Negro votes throughout Ohio should Lausche fail to endorse Stokes, and Gilligan became one of the first statewide Democratic candidates to recognize and solicit the black political power that Stokes had generated.

Stokes, while he naturally coveted Lausche's support, did not openly seek it. He had become committed to no one yet in his race for mayor, and he was wary of

Lausche. John Gilligan was more his type of Democrat and he wanted to preserve his options, as great society Democrats sometimes like to say. The cosmo votes, so decisive in so many Cleveland elections, might yet be decisive in 1967, and Stokes had been weakest in those wards.

In 1965, in ward 14, for example, Stokes had received only 74 votes out of a total of 6,669 cast. In ward 15 he had got only 81 out of 6,877. In ward 9 there had been only 224 Stokes votes out of 11,786. In the primary in 1967 he had increased these figures to 710 in ward 14, 487 in ward 15, and 1,112 in ward 9. He was clearly making inroads, but he had attracted less white support here than on the west side, where he had been provided with forums and had been able, as he put it, "to show them I speak English and don't have two heads."

The cosmo voters were still not entirely convinced about either of those propositions.

The Negro voters' loyalty to Stokes, meanwhile, had increased to a near unanimity never approached in white wards. In 1965, Locher had had some support in those areas of the city: 346 votes in ward 17, 391 in ward 24, and 411 in ward 25, to Stokes's 4,617, 7,413, and 8,555. By 1967, all that Locher had left in those wards were 68 votes in ward 17, 128 in ward 24, and 118 in ward 25. But not even every Negro vote in the city would assure victory for Stokes if he lost a substantial portion of his white primary vote to Taft. Lausche had endorsed one Taft in 1950, and there was nothing, certainly not Democratic-party loyalty, to prevent him from endorsing a second in 1967.

Stokes was still looking for a way to crack the ethnic bloc, and then along came *Szabadsag*. That's right, *Szabadsag. Szabadsag* means "liberty" in Hungarian, and is the name of a daily newspaper published in both Hungarian and English, and its editor and publisher, Zoltan Gombos, printed a front-page editorial on October 14 endorsing Carl B. Stokes for mayor. Carl Stokes cannot read Hungarian, but he enjoyed that editorial, in both versions.

Szabadsag has a loyal and devoted readership, but it is mostly Hungarian. Stokes headquarters thought it would be a shame to withhold such beautiful prose from Poles, Ukrainians, Slovenians, Croatians, Rumanians, and, in fact, anyone who could read any language. Accordingly, the large Cleveland dailies, in page-length ads, were soon carrying:

> An important message for every Clevelander of foreign ancestry (which means all of us).
>
> Zoltan Gombos, well-known Cleveland civic leader, is editor and publisher of *The Szabadsag,* Hungarian-language daily newspaper. *Szabadsag* means "liberty." Keenly aware of the liberty and opportunity he obtained by migrating to America from his native Hungary, Zoltan Gombos—from his heart—wrote an editorial which he published on the front page of *The Szabadsag.* It is an editorial which every Clevelander—and every American—should read and ponder . . .

Then followed a reprint, in full, of the editorial, which praised Carl Stokes effusively and urged his election. But even better than the endorsement was the ingenious manner in which the editorial contained what appeared to be the implicit agreement of Senator Frank J. Lausche with everything that Zoltan Gombos was saying. It was the first time in his political career that Frank Lausche had been outflanked.

FOR MAYOR
    CARL B. STOKES
      —EDITORIAL—

Our city from its earliest history has been the melting pot of all races, where people of different nationality and cultural backgrounds could live together in peace and harmony. Cleveland has been good to the immigrant. Free from class distinctions and discriminations, he could settle down here, find a job in his trade or pursue his profession, own a home, raise a family, and give his children the kind of education that he himself could not get in the old country. He could also extend a helping hand to his brethren in his native land. Not the least, he could practice his religious and political beliefs without fear.

Cleveland has had many firsts, especially in the political field. This was the first major city where the so-called "ethnic" groups broke through the barrier of prejudices to elect outstanding members of their community to high public offices in the judicial and the administrative branches of our government. This was the first major city to elect a man of ethnic background, *Frank J. Lausche,* the son of humble but proud immigrants, as its mayor. This city also gave the inspiration and impetus to Lausche to be the first man of ethnic background and of Catholic faith elected governor and later U.S. senator of the great state of Ohio.

The citizens of Cleveland will have the opportunity to be a first again among the major cities by electing a Negro, Carl B. Stokes, as their mayor and thereby demonstrating to the free world and to free men everywhere that they have none of the very prejudices that forced them or their parents to leave their native country and settle in our city. They can prove that "equal opportunity" are not just empty words.

Carl B. Stokes is a man of extraordinary ability. He is a man of extensive legislative and administrative experience. He is a man who, in our estimation, can supply the dynamic leadership which Cleveland needs to regain its lost place in the front ranks of the progressive, forward-looking, growing American communities. Under his leadership, rebuilding and revitalizing of the city can be accomplished and the trend toward the suburbs can be reversed.

Under Carl B. Stokes's leadership Cleveland can fully live up to its reputation as a city where all races, creeds, and nationalities can live and prosper side by side; where industry and labor can coexist free of strifes; where equal opportunities are offered for higher education. Under his leadership all of us can live up to the ideals that inspired the ethnic groups to settle in Cleveland in their search for freedom and in pursuit of happiness. For these very obvious reasons Carl B. Stokes should be elected as the next mayor of the City of Cleveland.

This was strong medicine for readers in ethnic neighborhoods who had been taught to hate and fear those people in the next ward who were trying to move into *their* neighborhoods and to go to *their* schools. Stokes poll watchers in the ethnic wards had returned to headquarters primary night discouraged and depressed by the grim determination with which the voters there had voted not so much for Locher as against Stokes.

One bemused poll watcher told of the very old lady who had to be helped into the polling place and then, being unable to read English, had to be helped to mark her ballot. She was asked how she wanted to vote, and replied, "To keep it like it is," meaning Locher. The Stokes witness knew that this procedure violated the election laws and that she should have challenged that vote. But she was a Ph.D. in English (one of thirty Ph.D.'s among the Stokes volunteers), with the sensitivity of a poet, and if this poor old lady wanted to struggle down to the polling place to vote her prejudices, she wasn't going to stop her. Ph.D.'s do not make good challengers.

So in ward 7 they wanted "to keep it like it is," and next door in ward 12 they wanted "to tell it like it is," and ward 7 and ward 12 seemed miles and years apart.

But Carl Stokes believed that ward 7 and ward 12 could rebuild the city together, and now, apparently, so did Zoltan Gombos. And the editorial had invoked the name of Frank J. Lausche. The battle for the cosmos had begun.

The Hungarian Freedom Fighters Circle decided they would rather switch than fight, and after having endorsed Democrat Locher in the primary, switched to Republican Taft in the general election. But the Freedom Fighters were more than balanced by the Alliance of Poles of America, which came out for Stokes.

The Alliance was apparently *unallied* with their womenfolk, because the Polish Women's Association immediately endorsed Taft. Stokes headquarters countered with an announcement of an All Nationalities Committee for Stokes, whereupon Taft's office announced that he now had on *his* committee a Croatian, a Greek, a Lebanese-Syrian (whether this meant two people or one is unclear), a Russian, a Serb, a Slovak, a Slovenian, and a Ukrainian. But Taft had failed to come up with a grand-sounding name like All Nationalities Committee.

Zoltan Gombos had displeased the Freedom Fighters. Their spokesman announced: "We're quite disturbed about the recent endorsement of Stokes by the Hungarian newspaper *Szabadsag*. The paper's endorsement does not express the opinion of the Americans here of Hungarian descent."

Nor, of course, did the Freedom Fighters express the opinion of American Hungarians. What was important to the election was who controlled the newspaper—and Zoltan Gombos did.

Seth Taft could have the Freedom Fighters, but as for Carl Stokes, give him *Szabadsag*—liberty.

17. THE DEBATER

THOUGH Taft is a famous name in Ohio, Seth Taft wasn't sure that voters within the city limits of Cleveland knew who he was. The establishment surely knew, and the suburbanites, and the committees, foundations, and good-government groups. But he had only once run for public office prior to 1967, and that was in a race for the state senate in which he had been defeated. He had gone relatively unnoticed in the primary, all the attention having been focused on the Democratic race.

He now had to establish his identity with the Cleveland voters. They mustn't confuse him with his cousin Robert Taft, Jr., or his more distant cousin William Taft, serving in the Ohio legislature from one of Cleveland's Republican suburbs, or another distant cousin, Kingsley Taft, chief judge of the Ohio Supreme Court. He would not be confused with his father, Charles Taft, who, while a famous man, is little known to Cleveland voters, but there would undoubtedly be some out of touch these last thirteen years who might mistake him for his uncle, the late Senator Taft. It was doubtful that anyone would confuse him with his grandfather. For one thing, he is much thinner. Seth Taft has a lean, hungry look and the serious, sincere manner of a man intent on doing good, and he *has* done good on numerous civic and governmental committees, on study groups, on foundation boards, on community action bodies—he has done everything, and more, that society demands of a high-born, wealthy, ivy-educated, socially responsible pillar of the community.

Taft's wife, Frances, had also been busy doing good, having been almost as active in the community as Seth. But, at the same time, she is a very outspoken person with little regard for what a candidate's wife should or should not say. During the campaign she was quoted in a newspaper as having remarked in regard to her children's brilliant educational record: "They come from a family where education is more important than having five pairs of shoes"—a remark hardly calculated to win votes in the ghetto where children have neither shoes nor an education.

And at a time when Seth Taft was being liberally sprinkled with jokes and criticism for presuming to run for mayor of Cleveland while still a resident of Pepper Pike (all three Democratic candidates had overworked this theme in the primary, and Senator Young had called Taft a rich Pepper Piker, an alliteration that was probably irresistible), Frances Taft said that they would have to think about moving back to Pepper Pike if her husband lost the election.

And so, forty-four-year-old Seth Taft, though well known to the establishment, was not nearly so well known to the voters as was his younger but more worldly opponent. It was indeed a strange reversal of roles. The invisible man had become so visible that the man from the power structure was desperate for attention. And so he challenged Stokes to a series of four debates to be locally televised.

Stokes, early in the campaign, had decided to make as many television appearances as possible. Many of the people whose votes he would be seeking had never talked with a Negro and possibly never hoped to. If he was going to reach these people (and he was determined to), it would have to be through television.

Some skeptics failed to appreciate the power of the kind of charisma Carl Stokes has. One former Clevelander now living out of town responded to a fund appeal from a Stokes supporter with a check and the perhaps facetious remark: "My advice on running a Negro candidate would be to keep him on radio and off television."

But, as Stokes himself had noted, everyone in town

certainly knew he was a Negro. What he had to do, then, was let the people know what kind of a man this Negro was and what he stood for, and this he had done superbly in his television appearances. If the medium is indeed the message, then Carl Stokes has got the message. He is quite capable of sharing political prime time with such TV political stars as Edward Kennedy, Ronald Reagan, John Lindsay, and Charles Percy.

There is an old political maxim to the effect that the better known candidate should do nothing to give his opponent public exposure he could not get through his own appeal. Discarding that maxim, as he had many others, Stokes readily agreed to the debates, though he limited the number to two rather than the four proposed by Taft. After all, there was no point in giving him too much exposure (though later he agreed to two additional debates).

Stokes thought the debates necessary to prove to the public (and perhaps to himself) something on which no judgment had yet been made. It was generally conceded by most of Cleveland that Stokes was a more attractive candidate than Taft. He was better-looking, had more presence and charm, and was a much more effective and forceful speaker. It was also quite clear that Stokes was a better politician, had more governmental as well as more practical experience. Stokes now wanted to prove that he was also smarter than Seth Taft. Though he could not match Taft in breeding, background, money, and education, he wanted to demonstrate that he could more than match him in intellect, and that if Cleveland chose him for mayor, it would be electing the candidate who was the best man in every relevant respect.

Taft had told Cleveland's voters that he had been a Phi Beta Kappa at Yale; that his wife was a Phi Beta Kappa too, and his oldest son; that two of his other children were merit scholars. He could have recited the educational credentials of his younger brother, Peter, a Washington lawyer who had come to Cleveland to help in the campaign and who was introduced by Taft the night Cleveland's political history may record as Phi Beta Kappa night, but he let it go at that.

Stokes's academic background was somewhat different. A high school drop-out, he had attended (in fits and starts) a series of second-rate schools. But his education had not stopped there. He had already begun learning the art and science of politics and government. His post-graduate school had been the city. He knew the Union Club and the men who ate *filet mignon* there, and he knew the Lancer and the brothers who dined there on soul food. Everything he could find on the city and its problems he read and digested. He had not only studied the urban crisis, he had lived it, and therefore knew he could deal with it better than Seth Taft, Phi Beta Kappa notwithstanding.

Carl Stokes and Seth Taft had traveled a long way on widely divergent routes to reach the same platform in 1967. Their grandfathers, at the beginning of the century, had lived in an America in which it seemed un-likely that a Taft and a Stokes could ever meet, let alone compete. Now Carl Stokes was about to show that two generations of breeding in his family since that time had produced a Stokes who could compete on any level with the grandson of the man who could never have known Carl's grandfather, except, perhaps, as a servant.

After some preliminary skirmishing between the Stokes staff and the Taft staff, the ground rules for the debates were agreed upon. The Kennedy-Nixon debates were carefully studied and each headquarters was determined that its man should be the Kennedy of the two. Taft was to have the choice of an east-side location (in Stokes country) and Stokes the choice of a west-side location (in Taft country). The format, which, of course, was not that of a debate at all, provided for twenty-minute formal discussions by the candidates on issues of their own choice, plus a five-minute rebuttal period for each and an open question period.

The programs were to be taped for television viewing later in the evening of each debate. Whether in deference to the historical significance of the campaign, or whether simply because of convenience, each candidate chose a site with a historic, if not necessarily relevant, name. Taft chose Alexander Hamilton Junior High School in a predominantly Negro neighborhood, and Stokes selected John Marshall High School in the white west side. Both sides were to send enthusiastic supporters to each debate, some with loaded questions prepared in advance and all with an excess of zeal for their respective candidate. These partisans, however, proved to be more an embarrassment for their candidate than a harassment for his opponent.

It all had the air of a high school basketball game, with straw-hatted boosters of the candidates waving banners and signs, whistling, stamping, and booing. Unwary citizens who came to hear the debate and, hopefully, to be informed, must have wondered if they had wandered by mistake into some strange new interscholastic competition, played on a home and home basis in which the student bodies of Alexander Hamilton and John Marshall tried to outshout each other.

It would have been much less nerve-wracking for the candidates, and much more informative for the public, if the discussions had taken place in a quiet television studio, before a panel of questioners and without cheerleaders. But the idea of a town-hall-type meeting had seemed exciting at the time. (It would be too much so the evening of the second debate.)

Louis B. Seltzer, retired editor of the *Cleveland Press,* had agreed to act as moderator, and this seemed only appropriate, since, for thirty years as editor of the *Press,* Seltzer had listened to the arguments of Cleveland's mayoral hopefuls as they called at his office to seek his blessing. Seltzer had become known as Cleveland's king maker because of the strong support the *Press* had given to all the city's mayors since Frank Lausche's time. Under Seltzer's direction, the paper tried to mother Cleveland like a hen with her brood—scolding, cackling, nagging, and generally scratching up a lot of dirt and dust in the barnyard. In the Sam Sheppard murder case, the *Press* had even gone so far as to act as police, prosecutor, judge, and jury; but, when the Supreme Court reversed the conviction (after Sheppard had been in prison for ten years), it became apparent that these functions could better be handled by duly designated public officials, and since that time, more so since Louis Seltzer's retirement two years ago, the *Press* has generally been more permissive in letting Cleveland run its affairs, restricting itself, more or less, to reporting them.

Louis Seltzer's function as moderator was to explain the ground rules to the audience, tell the speakers when their allotted time had expired, select the questions from the audience, and try to maintain a semblance of order in the Alexander Hamilton Junior High auditorium, which was hot, being overcrowded with one thousand unruly, mostly partisan Clevelanders, and which had a faulty loud-speaker system that almost ended the great debate before it had begun. Finally, the windows opened, the loud-speaker repaired, the boosters and hecklers temporarily quieted, the debate was ready to begin. Once again, as so many times in the past, candidates for mayor were appearing before Louis Seltzer to present their arguments. But this time he was not the king-maker— only the time-keeper.

Seth Taft lost the flip of the coin (it would be nice to know if it was a Lincoln penny or a Kennedy half-dollar), and Stokes elected to speak last.

Grimly serious, Seth Taft leaped right to the attack. He knew that he could not match Stokes in forensic skill (as a prosecutor Carl Stokes had tried hundreds of criminal cases, while Taft had rarely, if ever, been inside a courtroom) or in wit or charm (Taft is an intelligent man who knows his own limitations) or in delivery (Taft, not an inspired speaker, tends to be pedagogical, and his speaking voice is weak and high-pitched, unlike Stokes, who can deliver a speech like Harry Belafonte can deliver a song). He had decided to expand on the themes he had used in his radio spot announcements: (1) that Stokes dealt in generalities and not in specifics; (2) that he had sought outside help; and (3) that he had compromised on campaign pledges.

He wove all these themes into his opening remarks, hoping that such aggressiveness from a gentlemanly, conservative, polite member of the establishment would unnerve Stokes. (Stokes had once told Taft that he [Taft] was not "tough enough to be mayor.")

> As a candidate for mayor, I am running on my programs to answer the city's problems. My opponent is running on his powers of persuasion.
> I think my ability to tackle the city's problems is good. My opponent's ability to persuade is good . . .
> Now he has a set of witty remarks for me, I know. The trouble is, Carl, all your opponents just let you get away with it. Nobody has reached up to pull you down. I think tonight—right now—is the time to do just that.
> You've been doing all the finger-pointing, asking all the questions. Tonight let's see you answer a few yourself. I'm going to ask you three:
> How many outsiders, and what are their motives, are behind your campaign?
> How about those compromises after the primary? You backed down on Bert Porter, Muny Light, and Shaker Lakes. Is Chief Wagner going to be next?

Do you intend to present a program? Or don't you think the people would understand?

Influence is pouring in from everywhere, from Washington, from anonymous high officials lending their backing. President Johnson has given his "full" support, Hubert Humphrey says he will be glad to come here personally to campaign for you.

And I am glad to know that you are going to get steak at the White House next week.

What is the reason for this Washington interest? Of course, they are worried about Cleveland—but more important at the moment, I fear, they are in political trouble themselves. And their interest at the moment is not in Cleveland.

If the President and Vice President wanted to do something about our problems here, where have they been all these years?

This really was not much for openers. Cleveland had expected more from a man like Seth Taft in his first direct confrontation with Stokes. He had, after all, spent many years on study committees and in civic groups trying to diagnose Cleveland's ailments, and it was thought he would concentrate on positive programs to cure those ailments. Taft did have a program, of sorts, but he was reluctant to start out with his proposals because they were substantially the same as his opponent's. It would have been a duet and not a debate had the candidates talked only about specific problems and specific remedies.

Seth Taft's rhetorical questions were to a large extent irrelevant, and to some extent dishonest. Stokes had not withdrawn his demand that Porter resign, and had not backed down on his promise to replace Chief Wagner. Nor had he changed his proposal to sell the Shaker Lakes or renegotiate the lease, and, of course, the reference to Washington was sheer demagoguery, since Seth Taft knew better than most that urban problems, if they are to be solved, need massive federal assistance. The only legitimate question dealt with Stokes's position with regard to the municipal light plant. The unions were not in favor of the sale, and so he had promised labor that if there were a sale it would be only after a referendum vote in which the people of Cleveland would determine the fate of Muny Light.

Stokes had insisted that the crisis of the city was so extreme that it was almost futile to talk in terms of specific proposals. What was needed, he had argued, was a whole new approach to urban problems, a new spirit of adventure, of boldness, of daring, of imagination. Taft could not play the same tune, and went on to make three specific proposals: a reorganization of the police department, the creation of branch city halls to provide a more responsive government, and a low-cost housing program.

Stokes had no intention of making the slightest reference to Taft's questions. He knew they would be asked by others in the question period, and he preferred to set his own mood and his own pace for his speech. Stokes opened with the classic and obligatory political ploy which Taft, in his political inexperience and lack of sensitivity to what those people out there are really thinking about, had completely forgotten. This debate represented the candidates' first television appearance since the primary election—the opening gun of the campaign—and Taft had completely forgotten to introduce his wife to the audience.

And so, before launching into his speech, Stokes asked the indulgence of those in the audience and those watching on television while he introduced those to whom, he said, he owed so much—and Shirley Stokes, with her lively face and photogenic smile, arose to resounding applause, as did handsome gray-haired Mrs. Louise Stokes.

Seth Taft's face sagged perceptibly, while, presumably, the television audience wondered if he had a family at all. There are cynics in Cleveland who claim that this lapse cost Taft more votes than anything that was to happen in the campaign. In this age of electronic politics, it is possible that that appraisal is not too far off the mark. There are serious students of politics who claim that Richard Nixon would have been elected President in 1960 had it not been for a perspiring forehead and a heavy beard under the strong lights of the first Kennedy-Nixon debate.

Taft tried to repair the damage at the next debate, two nights later, at which he again lost the coin toss and had to speak first. He introduced not only his wife, Frances, but also two of their children and his brother, Peter. But the damage had been done. By then the white people of Cleveland had had two days to reflect on what a nice man that Carl Stokes must be, even if he is colored, for thinking first of his wife and mother, and both of them looking so nice on television. But that Seth Taft, they might have thought, what a cold fish—hardly ever smiled, and didn't even introduce his family.

After the applause for his wife and mother had died down, Stokes turned to the audience:

> You, the people of Cleveland, must decide whether you want a city-hall administration that will act boldly, courageously, and successfully, a city administration that understands the problems of human beings in all walks of life, in all segments of society, an administration that will have a dedication to the people—or, an administration attuned to the remote security of Pepper Pike, led by a man who doesn't understand what it means to be hungry, unable to understand what it is for his children to be hungry, without shoes, without clothes, a man who has spent most of his life attending committee meetings; meetings which usually resulted in handsome, expensive reports— reports doomed to gather dust in unconsulted filing cabinets. . . .

> Carl Stokes has nowhere to escape. My family lives here. I must make the streets safe for your wife and children because then they will be safe for my wife and children. . . .

> What Carl Stokes offers Cleveland is a new spirit, a belief in people, a spirit of adventure, a spirit of dedication and determination, and the vigorous courage to do what has to be done to make Cleveland a model city for everyone.

> I hope you will appreciate my personal relationship with the federal government, despite the sarcasm of my opponent. We're going to need money, lots of it, to solve our problems. And I want every dime I can get from the federal government.

> One of my first duties as mayor will be to go to Washington to see Lyndon Johnson personally—in addition to the kind of talk we'll have next Thursday.

I'll see him to straighten out Cleveland's present urban-renewal mess, to win a quick restoration of the federal funds we need to rebuild our city, to help develop new low-rent housing and job-creating industrial parks.

Stokes then went on to criticize Taft for his provincialism in resenting attempts to seek help for Cleveland outside the city. He would seek help wherever he could find it, he said, and mentioned how he had discussed some of Cleveland's urban-renewal problems with Edward Logue, of Boston and Harvard, one of the country's foremost urban experts and an unsuccessful candidate for mayor of Boston in 1967. This led to speculation that Logue would be coming to Cleveland as urban-renewal director in a Stokes administration. Stokes did, in fact, offer the post to Logue after the election, and, while Logue refused the job, he has served as a consultant on Cleveland's renewal problems.

The first debate produced little to cause anyone to change his views or his evaluation of the candidates. In the question period Stokes had displayed more poise and rapport with the crowd, but that had been expected. Both men had been well informed and knowledgeable about city affairs, and tempers had flared only once or twice. No matter who won, Cleveland was certain to be the winner with two competent, highly qualified candidates to choose from. But the campaign promised to be a dull one. Taft and Stokes had known each other for years, and though they were not friends, they respected each other's abilities and intentions. Stokes had proved in the primary that white Clevelanders would vote for a Negro, and with the overwhelming Democratic majority in

Cleveland, plus the labor-union support, there really seemed to be nothing that could prevent Carl Stokes from becoming the city's next mayor. Nothing, that is, except race, and Seth Taft was not the kind of man who would conduct a campaign on a racial basis, or permit one to be conducted on his behalf.

Most Clevelanders thought that the primary election had removed the question of race from the 1967 campaign. But it was only the more blatant kind of racism that had been buried by the primary. It was, perhaps, presumptuous of Cleveland, and of Carl Stokes, and of Seth Taft to believe that the race question, which is foremost in the consciousness of everyone in this country, could be solved so easily in Cleveland, Ohio. Two nights later, it was clear that it had not been, and it was to be Carl Stokes who would unnecessarily raise the issue.

18. TWO GRANDSONS

IT WAS generally conceded that in mid-October, before the second debate, Carl Stokes was so far ahead of Seth Taft that he could have vacationed until election time and still have won by fifty thousand votes. That, in fact, was the edge that bookies were willing to give Taft supporters on Short Vincent, but even with the spot there was no Taft money on the street, as they say.

It did indeed look hopeless for Taft. Carl Stokes had more or less unified the Democratic Party; he had not only the AFL-CIO backing but also the support of the Teamster's Union. He would almost certainly get the endorsements of the newspapers. With all that going for him, his staff said, he should play it safe until the election and coast in as the winner.

All that could beat him now would be a mistake, and all he need do was avoid making one. Sound enough political advice, and ordinarily Carl Stokes would have taken it. But something had been bothering him about the campaign and his opponent, something that stemmed from a private meeting he had had with Seth Taft early in the summer of 1967. That meeting, and what it led to, is perhaps an indication that a Carl Stokes and a Seth Taft cannot yet understand each other.

Seth Taft, ever since he had migrated north from Cincinnati, had worried and fussed over the city of Cleveland much as Louis Seltzer had. Taft, of course, had done it in a quieter, more sophisticated way, and as a member of the establishment *and* a Taft, he had done it in a spirit of *noblesse oblige*. There was never any doubt in his mind as to his responsibility to serve on committees, form study commissions, analyze and prescribe for the city's problems. It was his duty to give the city, in whatever way he could, the benefit of his superior knowledge and training, his understanding of forces that move and control society. In the 1960's as that society, in Cleveland, threatened to fall apart at the seams, it became apparent to Taft that the shadow government of committees and study groups was having less and less impact and influence. Cleveland's direction could no longer be shaped by establishment committees. If Taft was to fulfill his obligations to society, he would have to take a more direct part in political activity.

From time to time in the 1960's there would be speculation about Seth Taft's running for mayor, and a newspaper editorial now and then suggesting that what city hall needed was a man like Seth Taft. But everyone knew that it would require a unique combination of circumstances to elect a Taft mayor of a Democratic city. Taft thought he saw those circumstances developing in the 1965 campaign when Ralph Locher and Ralph Perk had been the party candidates and Carl Stokes and Ralph McAllister the independents. Taft knew that Cleveland had been the loser in every respect in that election. First, because Locher had won, and it had become obvious that he was no man to solve Cleveland's problems. Second, because, in the end, the election had turned solely on the question of race, with no real consideration of the many issues and problems plaguing Cleveland. Taft had seen how the vicious whispering campaign of fear and slander had increased the bitterness and hostility between the races and frightened white supporters of Perk and McAllister into voting for Locher in order to save the city from what they called a Negro take-over.

Nor, Taft reasoned, would Cleveland have been the winner had Carl Stokes won in such a race. Taft had no doubt that Stokes would be a competent mayor, but if he had been elected as a result of a split of the white vote among three candidates, he would be open to the charge of representing only part of the city, and there would be little hope of curing Cleveland's problems under those circumstances.

As the time for filing nominating petitions for the 1967 campaign approached, Taft, as did virtually everyone in Cleveland, assumed that Stokes would again file as an independent. He disliked the idea of a three-man race with Stokes and Locher because it would almost surely be a repetition of the 1965 election, dissolving once again into a bitter, sordid racial campaign. That would be bad for Cleveland and bad for Taft. Furthermore, in such an election, he would have no chance of winning.

Taft decided to pay Carl Stokes a visit. So far as is known, no candidate for public office in this country had ever sat down in a private conversation with his opponent for that office and presumed to tell him how he should conduct his campaign. There is no doubt that he was doing it in good faith and with goodwill and in the sincere belief that what he was doing was in the best interests of Cleveland. (Charles Wilson really believed it when he said that what was good for General Motors was good for the country. In the same way, Seth Taft—in this instance, at least—really believed that what was good for Seth Taft was good for Cleveland.)

He reminded Stokes of the racial ugliness of the 1965 campaign. (Stokes, of course, had lived it—Taft had merely observed it from the seventeenth floor of the Union Commerce Building.) All that would be accomplished in a three-man race, he added, would be a continuation of the Locher regime, and Cleveland might not survive two more years of Locher. Furthermore, in a contest of this kind, the legitimate issues would be overshadowed again by the racial issue, preventing the kind of analysis of Cleveland's problems that was necessary if they were ever to be solved. And if Stokes filed again as an independent, he, Taft, having already announced that he would file as the Republican candidate, would withdraw and Stokes would have to meet Locher head to head in the general election. (Taft was unaware that Stokes had already promised the Democratic national committee that he would run as a Democrat, a fact he neglected to tell Taft. Unlike his visitor, Stokes does not believe in private heart-to-heart talks with political opponents.) And Locher would win, Taft said, no matter how low his prestige had sunk, because his supporters would not be at all reluctant to engage in a racist campaign. On the other hand, with Frank Celeste already in the Democratic primary (Celeste had been the first to publicly announce), Stokes stood an excellent chance of winning the primary, and then Cleveland would have the kind of campaign it needed and deserved. In a Taft-Stokes contest, the issues in a Cleveland mayoralty election would at long last be aired by two intelligent, informed candidates, race would be forgotten, and the city of Cleveland, regardless of which candidate won, would be the real winner. And, Taft went on, it was more likely than not that Carl would be the winning candidate, since, without the race issue, Cleveland's heavy Democratic majority would give Stokes the Democrat (not Stokes the Negro) a decided adventage over Taft the Republican (not Taft the white man).

Carl Stokes and Seth Taft are as free from prejudice and bigotry as it is possible to be in racially schizophrenic America, but it was impossible for these two men to understand each other in such a strange confrontation. They could, by honest application of reason and good-will, free themselves of their prejudices, or at least recognize them as such and deal with them accordingly. But they could no more free themselves of their attitudes and views of life than they could shed their skins. Each was still his grandfather's grandson, and though they had traveled long roads through widely different countries to reach their meeting place in Carl Stokes's office, to a large extent they had carried their grandfathers' attitudes with them.

Carl Stokes was shocked and he was hurt; but he kept these emotions under control as he listened patiently (he is a good listener) to Seth Taft. He committed himself in no way, though he suggested that Taft must hold the white people of Cleveland in low esteem if he was so certain they would not elect a Negro mayor. Taft said that he had not meant that at all but rather that in a race against Locher, prejudice would be exploited, whereas in a race against Taft, Stokes (with Taft's help) could overcome and break down the fears and prejudices of white voters. Stokes did not bother to point out to Taft the logical inconsistency of his argument. If Taft was so concerned with the political bitterness or abrasiveness of a three-man general election, why was he urging Stokes to enter a three-man Democratic primary? No doubt because Taft knew that was the only way he could become mayor. Let the Democrats heat up the race issue in the primary, and then Taft could coast to victory in the afterglow. The primary and the general were only one month apart, and the whites would stay stirred up long enough to carry him into office over Stokes. If Locher won the primary, so much the better for Taft. In that event everybody would support him—even the Negroes. They certainly wouldn't vote for Locher.

Taft left the meeting with much the same feeling with which he left many civic committee meetings he had attended with Carl Stokes, a man of high intelligence and goodwill, like himself, who would be certain to see, in time, that what Taft proposed was eminently sensible and reasonable.

Carl Stokes felt otherwise. He thought he had been patronized. But he could endure that, because being patronized by well-meaning whites is an experience that no Negro can escape in this country. Those like Carl Stokes who still have faith in the Democratic ideal accept being patronized, resent but tolerate it, and hope to change the attitudes that foster it. Those without faith in the system, those who have lost hope, are infuriated by it and become black nationalists.

What Stokes resented was that Taft, an establishment lawyer, an effete suburbanite, an armchair politician, thought he could outsmart Carl Stokes with such

a patently obvious political trick. But worst of all, and
something he could not forgive, was the apparent lack
of belief that Taft himself had in the democratic process.
If this President's grandson, who had gone to all the
right schools, learned all the right codes, lived by all the
right standards, believed that Cleveland, given a clear
choice between white and black, could choose only white
regardless of the merits of the candidates, then he really
had no more faith in the system than the black nationalists did. And a man with such little faith, Stokes thought,
who wanted badly enough to be mayor, could not be
able to resist a subtle, sly exploitation of racial feelings
He would watch Taft carefully, he resolved, and nail him
every time he attempted, ever so genteely, to capitalize
on race. It would be a difficult political concept to grasp.
Voters like their issues, if not their candidates, to be
presented in black and white, with no subtleties or sophis-
tications. He would much rather deal with the more
blatant type of bigotry of the Locher supporters. There,
at least, the image and the reality were identical. With
Taft he would have to get through the image to get to
the reality. He would have to show the people of Cleveland that Stokes believed in Cleveland even if Taft did
not.

Thus a new picture of Taft was being formed in Carl
Stokes's mind—a picture that was as tragically inac-
curate as the conception Seth Taft had of Carl Stokes.
Taft wanted badly to be mayor, but not badly enough to
do anything that violated the standards and codes by
which he had lived, and those excluded any form of

what he considered to be bigotry and racism. He was convinced that Carl Stokes was as concerned with the future of Cleveland as he was, and recognized the necessity of healing old racial wounds and preventing new ones. But Stokes believed that the future of Cleveland required a demonstration of Cleveland's faith in democracy. Taft felt the need of no such demonstration. Four centuries of American Tafts had been his living demonstration of democracy. All he wanted was for Cleveland to have a good mayor—and either Carl Stokes or Seth Taft would surely be a good one. It was impossible for a Taft to understand how a Stokes could want or demand more than that.

19. A BLACK AUTOMOBILE AND A WHITE MICKEY MOUSE

STOKES had been, perhaps, overly sensitive to expressions of doubt as to the possibility of a Negro mayor in Cleveland because of another meeting he had had, not long before, with a newspaper reporter. This reporter, probably Cleveland's keenest political analyst, had stated it as his opinion that Cleveland would not elect a Negro mayor in a man-to-man race even if the other candidate were nothing but "a white Mickey Mouse." Stokes, like all missionaries, is tolerant of heathen who cannot be expected to know better, but he is inclined to be impatient with those who presumably have expert knowledge of the democratic process without having faith in it. To the disbelievers, of course, it is simply political realism. To Carl Stokes, it is heresy.

He had been depressed by the reporter's remark and sadly reminded of it in that later "heart-to-heart" with Seth Taft. This certainty that the mayor's chair would continue to carry a *For Whites Only* label if one Negro ran against one white man was, of course, shared by all the "political realists" in town. The *New Yorker* magazine, for example, had quoted one Cleveland politician as having said that any campaign with a Negro candidate would be a racial campaign with the whites voting for their man and the blacks voting for theirs, whether he be "a black Muslim, a black dog, or a black automobile."

Carl Stokes refused to believe this, and in the face of the tensions that had arisen between the races, it required a true believer indeed to harbor any hope of racial harmony. In the wake of Cleveland's bitter school-segregation fight (which led to the rise and fall of Ralph McAllister), the Murray Hill riots, in which Negroes caught in Little Italy were attacked; the Hough riots, in which it was open season on Whitey's property, virtually everyone was direfully prophesying a long, hot summer for 1967.

Sporadic acts of violence did in fact occur throughout that summer, sometimes perpetrated by whites on blacks and sometimes by blacks on whites. In September, on East Ninety-seventh Street, in the heart of the Hough area, a group of young Mennonites from Pennsylvania, who for several years had maintained a settlement house providing playgrounds and summer camps for ghetto children, were beaten and driven out of the house by a group of young black nationalists. The Mennonites had been popular and well liked in the neighborhood, and the beating seems to have been motivated by nothing more than a blind hatred of Whitey.

And, of course, there were always the police. Not only the black community but also the United States Civil Rights Commission considered that department's citizen relationships to be among the poorest in the country. A so-called Little Hoover commission, appointed by Mayor Locher, had also severely criticized the department and had strongly suggested, though not specifically recommended, that the chief be replaced.

Carl Stokes knew that re-establishment of police prestige had to start with a new police chief, and Seth Taft himself had served on the Little Hoover commission and had made reorganization of the police department one of his basic campaign promises. Stokes was curious, therefore, as to why Taft had equivocated on the question of firing Chief Wagner. If Taft's campaign statements were to be believed, he would have to agree with what the Civil Rights Commission had found in its investigation of the Cleveland police department in April 1967, summarized in a report of the Ohio state advisory committee:

> Police have lost the respect of Negro residents in the Inner City who believe that police are discourteous and sometimes brutal, permit prostitution and gambling to

flourish, and discriminate in their treatment of white and Negro citizens.

Persons often are arrested without a warrant, without probable cause, and without an offense being committed in the presence of the police officer, and are detained for as long as 72 hours under a nonexistent charge known as "investigation" which makes them ineligible for bond.

Unlawfully detained persons are not charged with a violation of law, but, before being released, are told to sign a waiver. This waiver is a police-department form on which the signer admits to a charge, usually that of being a "suspicious person," and waives his right to sue the city for unlawful arrest and detention. . . .

Negro police personnel are assigned to predominantly Negro areas. There are only 133 Negroes on a force of 2,021; the highest-ranking Negroes are two sergeants. . . .

Seth Taft must have known that no improvement in citizen-police relationships could be expected unless Chief Wagner was replaced, yet he refused to include Wagner's dismissal in his platform—obviously in an attempt to gain those white votes Stokes might lose by his fire-Wagner promise. Carl Stokes, the almost complete politician, ordinarily could appreciate a tactic like that, being satisfied merely to point out the inconsistency of Taft's position, but his interpretation of what Taft had revealed about himself at their meeting now made Taft's reluctance on the Wagner issue seem like an attempt to exploit racial fear.

He began to see racial implications in everything Taft did, and Taft in turn began to accuse Stokes himself of exploiting the race issue. In his missionary zeal, Carl was out to cleanse the whole city of what he took to be the racist smog that was poisoning the air. But the smog was like Cleveland's air, and sometimes it was hard to tell the dirty smoke from an ordinary cloud. Many of the comments Taft made during the campaign were really innocent clouds; but they nevertheless seemed sinister to Carl Stokes.

At the very outset of the general-election campaign, Taft publicly urged his supporters to avoid making an issue of race in a statement called "Campaign Guiding Principles":

> Every individual is entitled to his own beliefs. However, when working on behalf of a candidate for public office, individuals must present only the beliefs of the candidate. A candidate can talk only to a limited number of people himself. I must rely on you to tell my story. It must be the real story and the same story all over the city.
>
> During the campaign careful attention to this guiding principle is necessary if I am to be successful in conveying my views and programs, particularly in view of the racial overtones that clouded the Democratic primary and the 1965 mayoralty election. The Cuyahoga Democratic party has issued a number of vicious statements concerning the candidacy of Carl Stokes, and others have conducted whisper campaigns.
>
> We cannot tolerate the injection of race into this campaign. As a supporter you should know the following facts:
>
> 1. I have stated in my program for the city that the No. 1 problem to be solved rests in the area of human relations.
>
> 2. I was author of the (1965) Ohio Fair Housing Law. This law says all people in the business of renting or renting and selling properties must make their listings available

to everyone regardless of race on a first-come, first-serve basis. This does not mean private citizens have to sell houses to anyone they don't want to. I believe a man's home is his castle. As mayor I would enforce the Ohio Fair Housing Law.

3. As mayor, I will see to it that the city's 12,000 jobs will be available on an equal-opportunity basis on all levels. This means I will not give the jobs to people because they are white and I will not give jobs to people because they are black. Nor will I fire any city employee who is doing a good job.

4. Concerning the race for mayor, I do not believe it will be decided by the race issue. Many people will vote for Carl Stokes because he is a Negro. Many people will vote for me because I am white. I regret this fact. I will personally work hard to convince people they should not vote on a racial basis. The deciding votes that both Carl Stokes and I will strive to reach are those—Negro and White—who will vote for the man they believe offers the best program for Cleveland. Just as the primary election was finally decided by such people, despite the disgraceful racial campaign conducted with vigor in all sections of the city, and what I say before one audience will not differ from what I say before a different audience. . . .

This high-sounding document, purporting to remove race as an issue in the campaign, had unmistakable racial overtones. Taft is too informed a man not to know that.

"I believe a man's home is his castle" has become the segregationists' battle cry. Just one year before, in Maryland, an unknown contractor named George Mahoney, who had never been elected to anything, won the Democratic nomination for governor of Maryland with a campaign based almost exclusively on the slogan "A man's home is his castle." The whites of Maryland knew what this meant—that George Mahoney would protect them from the Negroes. Mahoney's campaign, his slogan, its racial overtones, and its effectiveness were widely reported in papers and magazines. Though Mahoney was defeated in the general election, his campaign had been widely publicized and his slogan picked up and exploited by one more successful than he—Claude Kirk, now governor of Florida. And Taft surely knew that what that beautiful phrase meant in Maryland and Florida it meant in Ohio as well—"I won't let the Negroes take your home."

Stokes was being accurate, then, not hypersensitive, when he accused Taft of being less than honest in his so-called disavowal of the race issue.

"We cannot tolerate the injection of race into this campaign"; yet the Cuyahoga County Republican chairman, A. L. (Sonny) De Maioribus, seemed perfectly willing to tolerate it. The same issue of the *Plain Dealer* that carried Taft's "guiding principles" quoted Sonny as saying:

> Whether we like it or not, we don't want to inject race, color, or creed. But you must agree the inclination of Negroes is to vote for a Negro, and it's going to be vice-versa in white areas. There's no use kidding ourselves. We don't want to inject race, but it's there.

On October 17, the day before the second debate, Seth Taft made a campaign appearance that Stokes feared would revive racial emotions that had been aroused by a sensational Cleveland murder the year before.

On November 5, 1966, a thirty-year-old choir singer had been murdered in the early evening across the street from Severance Hall, where she was to attend a rehearsal. Severance Hall is in that area of Cleveland known as University Circle, which borders the Hough area and which contains most of Cleveland's museums, two of its universities, and the home of the Cleveland orchestra. During recent years the area had been the scene of many rapes, muggings, attempted assaults, and even a kidnaping. It was still considered a dangerous area for after-dark strolls, even though additional police protection and increased lighting had somewhat decreased the incidence of crime.

The victim, according to the police, had apparently got off the bus she had taken from her home and was walking toward Severance Hall when she was dragged from the sidewalk into the bushes and murdered. Her body had not been found until the following morning. That such a crime could occur early in the evening, unnoticed by the heavy automobile traffic on Euclid Avenue, Cleveland's main street, was particularly shocking to the community. The murderer has never been caught, but since most of the crimes in the area which had been solved had been committed by Negroes, there was an immediate, widespread assumption that this criminal too had been a Negro. Cleveland's racial fever had gone up a few degrees more.

It is an irony of big cities in America that depressed

areas should come so close to affluent ones and yet be so far away. University Circle is just such a wealthy community, with its well-endowed museums and universities—an island of culture surrounded by an angry sea of poverty and bitterness that is Hough.

In what must surely be classified as one of the most bizarre appearances of this or any other campaign, Taft, with his brother, two staff assistants, and five straw-hatted Taft girls, paid a ceremonial visit to the spot in University Circle where the body had been found one year before. This pilgrimage was duly reported in the newspapers and was perhaps what finally persuaded Carl Stokes to take the step that came to be regarded as his biggest mistake of the campaign.

From the beginning of the campaign, and especially since the primary, Stokes had been subjected to a constant and bewildering barrage of suggestions and advice from every professional and amateur politician in town and from many out of town. Most candidates for office, if they make themselves accessible to well-meaning friends, are the beneficiaries of much useless advice on how to win elections. The trick, of course, is for the candidate to isolate himself from his friends without alienating them, and to restrict his policy-making meetings to a small inner circle of advisers. Carl Stokes found it difficult to withhold himself because he had become a victim of his own technique. For years he had sought out friends and politicians and solicited their advice and opinions. His course of action, no matter what the subject, had almost always been determined beforehand in his own mind, but those to whom he had talked, believing they had helped him, felt obliged to continue to help him.

"Forget the racial issue," one would tell him. "You are way ahead now and all you have to do to win is to keep saying what a great place you're going to make Cleveland." "You must talk about the racial issue," another would say. "It is being talked about all over town in any event and you must get it out in the open."

"Don't be so witty and sarcastic about Seth Taft," was advice frequently given. "You are starting to make people sorry for him." This bit of advice might have had some merit. Stokes's presence on the platform completely overshadowed Taft, with his deadly serious committeeman-approach to problems. At one of their joint appearances Taft had unveiled a brand-new low-cost-housing scheme to replace the plan that Stokes had previously proven was impractical. Taft now proposed that five hundred acres of land owned by the city of Cleveland, but outside the city, be utilized for relocation of Clevelanders dispossessed by urban-renewal projects. Without bothering to comment on the merits or flaws of the plan, Stokes simply said: "I'm not going to say anything at all about all those people from Cleveland that Seth Taft wants to move next to the county workhouse."

Taft had either forgotten, not known, or didn't care that this property, completely surrounded by a suburban community, held the building in which all county prisoners serving terms for misdemeanor offenses were housed. Little more was heard of this Taft housing proposal.

"Be more specific in your programs," Stokes would be urged one day, and "Be more general," he would be told the next.

The advice he would most often receive from white councilmen, legislators, and assorted politicians was that he should appear less confident and self-assured ("cocky," they called it), less proud ("arrogant," they said). They apparently wanted him to conform to their constituents' ideas of what a Negro should be, and that was certainly not one who dressed expensively, spoke expansively, referred to himself in the third person in speeches ("Now what would Carl Stokes do about this problem?") and even sometimes used the royal "We."

One white officeholder with a Murray Hill following had flown all the way across the country two days before the unity meeting so that his excuse for being absent would have whatever veracity long distance would give to it. The advice he most frequently offered Carl was that he should be more 'humble." (One member of Stokes's staff who overheard this bit of counsel remarked to another: "What the hell does he want Carl to do, say 'Yassah Massah'?")

Stokes, of course, had learned to tune out on most of the advice he was getting. Politics was what he knew best, and he was his own best counsellor on traditional political problems. But there was no precedent or tradition to look to in a white-black contest for the office of mayor of a large city. Even his staff of able young lawyers, recruited from the best law firms in the city (including Jones, Day, Cockley, and Reavis) to prepare position papers and resumés of issues, had been unable to help him there. Race was the insoluble problem to them as it had been to everyone else. Most close observers of the political scene agreed with Stokes's own appraisal of himself as the more competent and qualified candidate and the one more likely to do the job that Cleveland needed. He would have liked to let it go at that, but of course he could not.

For one thing, he probably could not have become the nominee had he been white. Ironically, being a Negro, which had, at the outset of his career, kept him from his first political office, now seemed to be providing the impetus that would put him into office. If it had not been for his color, he would not have received all the nationwide attention in 1965 when he almost became mayor. That attention had made a national figure of him—among Negro groups, in any event— and his subsequent speaking engagements around the country had made friends for him, many of whom had provided valuable financial help in the campaign. If he had been white with a name like Stokes, there would have been no chance of his becoming mayor. Cleveland had only had one mayor since the time of Harold Burton in the thirties who had been neither a cosmo nor foreign born. The single exception had been Thomas Burke, but of course he was Irish, which was almost as good as being cosmo.

The nation would have paid very little attention to the nomination of another Democratic candidate in Cleveland, Ohio, but when Stokes became the nominee, both the nation and the world sat up and took note. In a way it was his color, not his qualifications, that had become significant. He had to deal with the election not only as Carl Stokes the candidate but also as Carl Stokes the symbol.

The press appreciated his unique position, seeing in the election more than simply a contest between two men. *Business Week* magazine had said: "But win or lose, his primary vote holds special significance both for Cleveland and for the nation."

And according to *Newsweek* magazine, ". . . the betting was that come November Carl Stokes would emerge the winner in the nation's tenth largest city—and a fresh symbol of the new chapter in U.S. urban politics."

A lot of people seemed suddenly to be counting on Carl Stokes for a great deal more than would be asked of his opponent—the difficult enough job of administering a city's affairs. His nomination seemed to most newspapers to be the most encouraging development in race relations in many years. The *New York Times* editorialized:

> . . . But when self-styled "militants" decry Negro-white co-operation as an impossible ideal and preach violence as a substitute for politics, Mr. Stokes's nomination is

encouraging proof that interracial cooperation and orderly progress through political activity are realities, not illusions.

Even the *Chicago Tribune* was encouraged:

By defeating the incumbent for the Democratic nomination for mayor of Cleveland, Carl B. Stokes illustrates yet again that Negroes can go far in the United States thru the orderly process of our society.

The *Tribune* could not resist lecturing just a little, however: "Stokes won his major-party nomination for mayor of one of America's largest cities not by demagogic pressure tactics but by persistent and patient improvement of his opportunities."

Ohio papers, of course, followed suit. The Dayton *Journal Herald* said: "Cleveland Democrats' election of Carl B. Stokes, a Negro, as their candidate for mayor is a great thing for the Negro in America and for the rest of us."

Carl Stokes is a man who knows himself well as a man and he is a man in full control of himself. He is not so sure of his direction as a symbol. It is uncharted territory. Yet, though he was uncertain of the role, he was proud of it, and decided to exploit the pride Clevelanders took in what the country was calling a reaffirmation of democracy. Cleveland needed something to be proud of and he had given it to them. No matter what fortuitous chain of circumstances had made it happen, it had happened first in Cleveland. If his nomination had given Cleveland's sagging morale such a shot in the arm, then his election would be a full-scale transfusion, and so he decided to appeal to the city's new-found pride.

In its first full-page ad following the primary, his headquarters had announced the unity rally in big boldface type:

LET'S DO CLEVELAND PROUD

Included in the ad was a reference to the political maturity demonstrated by Cleveland in the primary election, and the following statements:

"But when there are two steps to take, you don't relax after the first."

"Cleveland, again in unity, must go on to elect Carl Stokes as mayor."

This, it seemed to Stokes, was certainly a legitimate use of race in the campaign. The whole world had recognized his primary victory as a symbol of democracy. His own faith had been vindicated. A demonstration of faith in democracy was something to be proud of. What his ad was saying, in effect, was that Cleveland could be proud of electing the best man even though the best man happened to be a Negro.

That was not the same, he felt, as Seth Taft's using segregationist slogans like "A man's home is his castle" in order to suggest that Stokes was going to ruin neighborhoods, or his ostentatious parade to the scene of a tragic and frightening murder that could be nothing but an attempt to call up old racial fears and tensions.

Statements by Taft that ordinarily would have gone unnoticed by Stokes now took on an added dimension when related to what Stokes thought was Taft's confidence that Cleveland would not elect a Negro mayor. Finally, against the advice of Ken Clement, but with the encouragement of Al Ostrow, his P.R. man, Stokes decided to attack Taft on what he was convinced was Taft's exploitation of the racial issue. Stokes's inner circle of advisers had narrowed to Ostrow and Clement as the hard core. But they often disagreed, and Stokes's ultimate decision would sometimes agree with Ostrow's and sometimes with Clement's.

Ostrow, of course, was the P.R. man, and former *Cleveland Press* reporter, who had been provided for the campaign by Cyrus Eaton. In 1965, in a P.R. capacity, Ostrow had, on behalf of the Cleveland AFL-CIO, supported Locher. No one knows whether Stokes agreed to use Ostrow because of or in spite of his hand in that 1965 campaign.

In any event, Ostrow is a shrewd political observer and a successful P.R. man. There was a tendency among some Stokes supporters to blame Ostrow for what they called the second debate fiasco, but if the fault was anyone's, it was the candidate's. Considering the fact that Stokes was the target of a daily stream of poisonous letters, many of them threatening violence on him, and that he was bombarded constantly with a bewildering barrage of advice on how to handle the race issue, and considering his central role in a unique American political experience, it is a remarkable tribute to his taste, tact, judgment, and wisdom that he made only one major mistake. It might even have proved to be a wise move if a different forum and a different form had been chosen for his accusation against Taft. The atmosphere at John Marshall was decidedly hostile to Carl Stokes on the night of the second debate—October 19. For once his supporters were outnumbered and outshouted. Stokes was later to tell a friend, "I could actually feel the waves of hate coming from the audience." He was facile enough to abandon a prepared speech and direct himself to other matters (and he had often done so), but he was determined to proceed with the plan he and Ostrow had developed.

Taft, once again the first speaker, once more accused Stokes of bringing outside influence into the campaign.

> Last Monday I asked you the motives behind all those carpetbaggers that are sending money from places like New York penthouses and Hollywood. People like Sammy Davis, Jr., I'm sure you remember.

The reference to Sammy Davis, Jr., impressed Stokes as yet another bit of subtle racism, especially since he didn't even know Davis. True, it was Jim Brown *and* Sammy Davis, Jr., who were responsible for the Stokes fund-raising party, but then why didn't Taft refer to Brown, a popular name in Cleveland and a man known to be Stokes's friend? Why not indeed, when he could use Sammy Davis, Jr., with a white wife and all! *There* was a name to make the hair rise on the back of any red necks in the audience.

Stokes paid little attention to the rest of Taft's speech. He was impatient to expose, once and for all, what he was convinced was Taft's basic lack of belief in the people of Cleveland and his reliance on their prejudice to defeat Stokes. His message was really quite simple and to the point: he believed in Cleveland, and was confident that its people could rise above the race issue. Taft did not believe, and how could such a man be a good mayor?

This charge had, in fact, been suggested by Stokes during the question period in the first debate two nights earlier. Litigation pending in Pepper Pike, in which Taft's home was located, had accused property owners there of restricting transfers in an attempt to exclude Negroes and Jews. Taft had denied the charge, but Stokes had then cited the law suit as a way, not of accusing Taft of bigotry, but of suggesting that perhaps he should stay home in Pepper Pike and cure that city's problems before trying to tackle Cleveland's.

A young Negro girl had then asked Taft: "If you are partial to Jews, what is your stand on Negroes?" (That is the way she put her question. It is impossible to say what she meant.)

Taft was visibly distressed as he answered:

I have spent twenty years in Cleveland and I have never had that asked of me before. I have worked on human relations. Just because I am running against Carl Stokes is no reason to call me a bigot. There are Jews on my street.

This was one of the very few references to Jews in the entire campaign. It is just as well. Anti-semitism is almost as slippery a subject as racism, and as impossible to grasp and hold down in a political campaign. There are, in any case, approximately only five hundred Jews still living within the city limits of Cleveland—too few to become an issue in the campaign. Besides, the candidates had quite enough trouble without them.

There was not a chance of anyone's understanding what Stokes meant by Taft's "racism." And in order to make his meaning understood, he would have to reveal, not just the private conversation months earlier with Seth Taft, but also that with the political reporter. And the whole argument was too subtle. Nevertheless, he tried.

> I am going to be brutally frank with you and equally frank with Seth Taft. The personal analysis of Seth Taft and the analysis of all competent political experts is that Seth Taft may win the November seventh election for only one reason. The reason is that his skin happens to be white.

After this somewhat melodramatic beginning, Stokes had intended to carefully and patiently explain how he had reached this conclusion. But it was several minutes before he was able to continue. Boos and jeers filled the auditorium. Louis Seltzer, who had never had this kind of trouble down at the *Cleveland Press,* finally succeeded in restoring at least partial order.

Stokes continued, somewhat shaken:

> On this question, which I could have avoided so easily

but brought out in the open for you to see, Seth Taft has pretended to bypass the so-called black-white issue. . . .

But in practically every public utterance he has made during his campaign, he not so subtly points out "Carl Stokes has more experience at being a Negro but Seth Taft has more experience at being a white man!"

Now, if this is not some kind of subtle appeal to race prejudice, then why does he continually bring this up? On October third the voters of this city clearly demonstrated by their votes in the Democratic primary election that they are more concerned about a man's ideas and ability than they are with the color of his skin.

So that issue has been resolved in this city.

But that very demonstration by the electorate is the very thing that has frightened Seth Taft in desperation to become mayor.

Because he never believed as I did and do, that the white electorate of Cleveland would vote for a person who happened to be a Negro.

Again he was drowned out by boos and catcalls. Quieting the crowd, he said: "If you don't agree with me, that's what ballot boxes are for."

Seth Taft is not a racist; Seth Taft is not a bigot. But he does not believe that the people of Cleveland can rise above the issue. He believes that any white candidate could beat Carl Stokes in the election.

How do I know this is true? Because Seth Taft told me.

Stokes then began to describe his private conversation with Seth Taft. But it was too late; he had lost the crowd. His plan had backfired.

It was a plan poorly conceived and poorly executed. Had he meant to expose Taft's "racism," there were better examples he could have used—the segregationist slogan and the murder march, for instance. He compounded his mistake by relying on still another private conversation, to support his claim that "all competent political experts" agreed that Taft could win only on the race issue. But this was only one reporter, not "all competent political experts," and, at that, could hardly be expected to win favor with the press, since, if Stokes was criticizing Taft for his exploitation of the race issue, he was also criticizing the reporter on the same basis.

The public was as bewildered as Taft, and their sympathies seemed to be with his simpler argument:

> Well, well, well! It seems that the race issue is with us. I was charged at Carl Stokes's campaign opener of bringing up the race issue.
>
> It now appears that if I say something on the subject, it is racism. If Carl Stokes says something it is fair play.
>
> "Don't Vote for a Negro: Vote for a Man!" he says in his ads. I agree with that. After the primary, the theme changed to "Let's Do Cleveland Proud." What has Cleveland done that makes it so proud? Nominated a Negro for mayor. Now it is "Do something proud by electing one."
>
> It is impossible to ignore this issue, but I have not brought it out once in the debates. I had no intention of bringing it up. The reverse is true. If Carl Stokes talks about it, nobody else can.

There was much public reaction to this debate—most of it unfavorable to Carl Stokes. The *Plain Dealer* wrote:

On major campaign debates between Carl B. Stokes and Seth C. Taft, the score is 1–1. Not one victory apiece— one loss.

Debates are more often lost than won and the two major clashes Monday and Wednesday were no exception.

Taft lost Monday, as the analysts had expected he would, because the Stokes personality came across much stronger than the Taft straight-man act.

But the result Wednesday was not what the pros expected. They figured to see a repeat performance of the Stokes charm-school course. Instead, Stokes made what many consider a major tactical error and came off second best.

Taft supporters, who had been dispirited after the first debate, suddenly became hopeful. His campaign headquarters were besieged by telephone calls on the day following the second debate. All the calls, they said, were from Democrats who had been offended by Stokes's racial argument, and from that point on, race became almost the only issue in the campaign. Almost, but not quite. Taft, realizing that his so-called program to cure Cleveland's crisis of human relations had not exactly excited Cleveland's voters, decided to attack Stokes personally.

He had discovered that in addition to Stokes's Cleveland home and the Shaker Heights home he had bought for his mother, he was also the owner of a rental property in the adjacent city of East Cleveland. That property, Taft learned to his delight, had several outstanding building-code violations against it, and Taft accused Stokes of being an absentee landlord who could not even maintain his own property, let alone halt the deterioration of Cleveland's neighborhoods. ("Deterioration of neighborhoods" was a catch phrase often used by Taft. It holds special significance for frightened white voters.)

Not only was Stokes an absentee landlord, charged Taft; he was also an absentee legislator, since, in the most recent session of the Ohio legislature, he had missed more roll-call votes than any other member of the Cuyahoga County delegation. Finally, Taft would also accuse Stokes of being an absentee Democrat, since he had more often fought the party than co-operated with it. Stokes for a while ignored these charges, but when it became obvious that they were having an impact on the voters, his campaign began to take a defensive turn. He claimed that his rental property was in the hands of a management company, and that he had therefore assumed the violations had been corrected. He defended his legislative record by arguing that the mark of a legislator is not his attendance record but what he accomplishes, and produced a letter he had received from Seth Taft in June 1967 commending him for his "excellent" work in the legislature.

But the tide seemed to have turned, and the Short Vincent bookies, who in mid-October had made Stokes a four-to-one favorite, were now quoting even-money odds, and both the *Press* and the *Plain Dealer* were predicting a very close race. Perhaps for the first time victory began to seem a real possibility to Seth Taft, and he apparently sanctioned a looser interpretation of his "Campaign Guiding Principles." Though he had discharged from his campaign committee several workers caught in the act of making flagrant racial appeals to white voters, he permitted, and attempted to defend, an inflammatory letter sent in his behalf to 45,000 members of various nationality groups. This letter, which prompted Stokes to accuse Taft of stooping to a "Louise Day Hicks appeal," contained most of the slogans and clichés which have come to symbolize urban racial tension. The letter urged the nationality voters to support Taft in order to "protect our way of life and to protect Cleveland, the citadel of nationalities in America." "Taft and Taft alone can give Cleveland back to the law-abiding citizenry." The letter, on official Taft nationality committee stationery, talked of "false charges of police brutality."

There was no doubt now that race had become the sole issue of the campaign. And whichever candidate had been ultimately responsible for that, it was now clear that most whites would vote for Taft and most blacks would vote for Stokes. And deep down below the surface, in the sick soul of some unhappy madman, a last desperate letter was conceived and sent to several thousand homes in the Murray Hill and Collinwood sections on the day before the election. Seth Taft surely knew nothing about it, but on election day the news of the letter spread rapidly through the Negro community. It read in part:

STOKES IS BLACK POWER

VOTE RIGHT————VOTE WHITE

You can rest assured that if Stokes is elected mayor of Cleveland you will get Negroes for neighbors and your children will have niggers for playmates. . . .

Fellow white Americans—This is not an election between the Republicans versus Democrats—this is a war between the niggers and the whites. All of the niggers and nigger lovers are voting for Stokes. Don't be a Judas to your own race. If the niggers win, it will be taken as a signal in Washington by Johnson to raise your taxes and spend more and more on the niggers and less and less on the white man and his children. If the nigger Stokes wins, it won't be safe for your women and children to walk the streets. Don't let the kikes from Shaker Heights and Cleveland Heights and the niggers run your city.

Get out and vote—vote—vote—for Taft!

20. A NIGHT IN BUDAPEST

I T WAS, perhaps, inevitable that race should have been the only topic of the campaign capable of generating any excitement. Not only because of the volatile nature of the subject, but also because the candidates, in their views on specific issues, their plans for Cleveland, and their basic conceptions of the nature of city government, were very much the same.

It was clear that whichever was elected, the reign of Cleveland's caretaker mayors had ended. Both men were aware that Cleveland was a sick city and both were prepared to prescribe radical remedies.

Both had spoken of the necessity of going outside the city to secure the best available manpower to boost Cleveland's urban-renewal program. This may not seem like much, but in xenophobic Cleveland, it would have been political suicide not many years ago to suggest that any aspect of Cleveland government be entrusted to non-Clevelanders.

Both proposed a radical reorganization of the Cleveland police department and both opposed a civilian-review board.

Both agreed that a Playboy Club might be a good thing to liven up downtown Cleveland. (*Anything* can become an issue in Cleveland politics. The Bunnies got into the act because Ralph Locher had once expressed opposition to a downtown urban-renewal proposal that included a projected Playboy Club in one of its buildings.)

Both agreed on the need for extreme measures to combat Cleveland's polluted air (Cleveland ranks as the fifth most polluted city in the United States), and both agreed to clean up the shores of Lake Erie. Name an urban problem and Cleveland had it and also two candidates who could discuss it at length. Two men who, measured by ideological standards, could have been running on the same ticket.

Measured on the traditional liberal-conservative scale, they also occupied the same general area of the political spectrum. In some respects, in fact, the Republican seemed to be to the left of the Democrat. His insistence that the city should continue to own and operate its municipal light plant, for example (a position he had reversed since 1965), was inconsistent with Republican dogma about getting the government out of business.

His position on public housing also seemed to lean more on direct participation of the city, whereas Stokes saw the city more as an agent for making public land and renewal funds available for private construction and rehabilitation. Stokes also took what might be considered a more conservative stance on law and order in the streets:

> Law and order does have to be preserved. I tell those who want to complain that violence in the streets is not the answer.
>
> Now suppose Carl Stokes were mayor and a riot happened. This is one reason I co-sponsored what is called the Anti-Riot Bill, which gives the governor the right, when a crisis is impending—not after there is looting and fire-bombing—to move in on his own and send in the national guard.

Stokes, always feeling the need to reassure anxious whites, even felt it necessary to promise a meeting of foreign newspaper editors that ". . . it just isn't so that Martin Luther King is going to run the city if I am elected." And though no one had asked him, he volunteered the information that "Stokely Carmichael and Rap Brown would not be welcome in my town."

Playing the role of the tough cop, Stokes ridiculed Taft's ability to stop crime in the streets:

You think this man is going to solve the problems of crime in our streets? He can't even solve the crime in Pepper Pike. The racketeers of this town aren't on Superior and Hough Avenue. They live in Pepper Pike and Gates Mills along with Mr. Taft.

Taft, on the other hand, did not feel the same need to wave the big stick. He seemed more the sociologist:

I have campaigned all over Cleveland on the ground that Cleveland is in the midst of a crisis of human relations. In sections where it is predominantly Negro, it is a crisis of racial relations.

We must attack this in the poverty areas, in unemployment areas, we must attack in the area of safety. Crime must be stopped.

It has been found that the common causes of riots in cities where riots erupted were jobs, safety, housing, and the conviction that nobody was listening.

It was, indeed, sometimes difficult to tell which candidate was which from their words alone. Seth Taft won much admiration, though few votes, by carrying his campaign to meetings of Negro groups. He was even brave enough to address a CORE meeting, where he stood among black-power signs and talked about "respect for law."

In the same city where just one year earlier the mayor had refused to meet with Martin Luther King, calling him an extremist, Seth Taft's appearance at CORE headquarters was indeed a milestone in Cleveland's political race relations. It might even have won him a few votes, since Carl Stokes is not nearly militant enough to be CORE's favorite candidate. But, though he gained in stature in the Negro community, Taft's visit with CORE probably cost him badly needed votes in the white wards. Though the CORE people listened respectfully to Taft's words, he could not have really communicated with them even if he had been speaking Swahili—which CORE, on the day of Taft's visit, had recommended be taught in Cleveland schools.

Taft, as determined as Carl Stokes to be a candidate of all the people, also made several walking tours through ghetto areas. As was perhaps inevitable, he was mistaken on one of these trips for Senator Taft, dead these thirteen years. But Taft had little chance of gaining significant Negro support, even among those voters who knew who he was and what he stood for. Had he been a reader of the *Call and Post,* he would have known that people whose votes he was soliciting had been told:

> Don't be fooled—
> Carl Stokes is not mayor of Cleveland yet!

— — — — — — — — — — — — — —

> Don't fall asleep and let the candidate from Pepper Pike—
> where people with "undesirable backgrounds" are barred
> by restrictive covenants—get into city hall!

To the slum voter, the election meant more than a simple choice between two men. Publisher William Walker's front-page editorial in the *Call and Post* had not even bothered to discuss the relative merits of the candidates: it was Carl Stokes against the white race:

CARL STOKES THE HOPE OF NEGROES—
A CHALLENGE TO CLEVELAND

Carl Stokes's candidacy for mayor of Cleveland represents the hope of all Negroes for status, recognition, and reward.

For over twenty-five years, the Negro vote in Cleveland has been the margin of victory for the Democratic party. In all of these years, the Democratic party has denied its full support to Negro candidates on its ticket except where they run in predominantly Negro wards or districts.

Negroes are tired of furnishing the votes for victory and not sharing in the rewards. Carl Stokes's candidacy is the inevitable desire by Negroes to share in their party's support for public office outside the ghetto areas.

Negroes are entitled to more than just the crumbs from the Democratic party's table. In the past, it has given its full support to Celebrezze, an Italian; Burke, an Irishman; Lausche, a Slovenian. So why not now a Negro?

If qualifications are not the yardstick, then what is?

Therefore, Carl Stokes's candidacy is a challenge to Cleveland. A challenge that the decent, fair-minded citizens can't ignore. It is not enough to say you are not a bigot: Cleveland must prove it at the polls. . . .

This editorial, like all of Walker's, was signed with the publisher's initials, forming an acronym appropriate for the emphatic tone of his newspaper—WOW. Nor was the *Call and Post* alone in its exhortations. Martin Luther King returned to town to tell black Clevelanders that voting in this election was a moral imperative and that God had commanded them to make a choice on election day. (He did not say which candidate God favored.)

One of the Cleveland radio stations with a predominantly Negro audience had its Negro disc jockeys, between the motown and the soul music, urge its listeners to get out and vote, to get "the burden off your back" and "put that cat into city hall." Again no candidate was specified, but no one has ever called Seth Taft a "cat." If the F.C.C. equal-time requirement were to be observed in Cleveland, there is at least one radio station that owes Seth Taft a week's free time.

Taft was clearly running against the wrong man. The degree of disillusionment with Ralph Locher was such that had Locher been Taft's opponent, Cleveland might now have a Republican mayor—something as rare for the present generation of Clevelanders as a Negro mayor. As Taft had shown, he was certainly no white Mickey Mouse.

Though to some it seemed that he had been bent on capitalizing on the race issue, Taft had, for the most part, campaigned against Carl Stokes in the same manner as he would have campaigned against Ralph Locher. The temptation to exploit racial fear to the fullest extent might have been irresistible to another candidate more desperate to become mayor. As it was, Taft resisted most of the pressures to shift the emphasis of his campaign, and Cleveland owes him a debt of gratitude. Other cities where black-white contests will inevitably occur will be fortunate if they have as one of the candidates a Seth Taft whose restraint, judgment, and basic decency can help calm a nervous city. Seth Taft had served his adopted city well, as he had done on so many committees.

The Stokes staff, convinced that their candidate could

only lose on the race issue, ran another full-page ad, but this time the message was less direct:

VOTE FOR SETH TAFT

(It would be so easy, wouldn't it?)
He's intelligent.
He has character. Honesty.
Sincerity.
A good education. A good background.
A good name.
But does he have the drive?
The boldness?
The imagination?
The basic experience and raw courage to lead this city to greatness?
We think the answer in this campaign is, that the man of drive, boldness, imagination, basic experience, and raw courage is named Carl B. Stokes.
And once you accept this, the rest is easy.

The "rest" presumably meant voting for a Negro. The Stokes P.R. and advertising staff was pushing this point so hard that some began to wonder whether Stokes really *did* believe. Since the second debate, Stokes had been under increasing pressure to avoid any further suggestion of the race issue. This ad was to further agitate those who had been exerting that pressure. Others on the staff thought the ad too cute. It seemed to them more Madison Avenue than Superior Avenue.

Madison Avenue was, perhaps, more appropriate, since, in this strangest of all campaigns, Carl Stokes, the Democrat with the wrong color and from the wrong side of the tracks, was getting as much (if not more) support from the business establishment as Seth Taft, the man with the right everything, one of the establishment's own. In addition to Cyrus Eaton, Stokes could claim as his campaign treasurer George Herzog, retired chairman of the board of the Union Commerce Bank, one of Cleveland's largest banks, and a retired vice-president of the Glidden Company as chairman of the Businessman's Committee for Stokes, which reminded Cleveland's businessmen that Carl Stokes had talked their language in the primary campaign:

"Maybe cities don't make profits," Stokes would tell them, "but they still need professional money-wise managers for such things as port authorities, urban renewal, and financial management. I intend to recruit experts from industry to come into city hall and help us out."

The business community was also aware that though Taft had had a grandfather in the White House, it was now Carl Stokes who went to dinner there and who would be the more likely one to bring a new influx of federal money into Cleveland. The prospect of this stimulus to Cleveland's economy made it easy for business leaders to say, as one did: "We're certainly overdue for a change. We sorely need better leadership, and I personally see nothing wrong with having a Negro mayor. We need a man who can get the job done."

With Cyrus Eaton, Cleveland's leading industrialist, and with George Herzog, one of Cleveland's leading bankers, as the nucleus, the business end of the Stokes campaign was indeed formidable. When money ran a little short toward the end of October, George Herzog was able to raise over $20,000 at a hurriedly convened dinner attended by only twenty businessmen.

A more impressive feat of fund-raising had been performed a few weeks earlier by some Stokes volunteers in the Negro ghetto, each of whom had asked five friends to donate *any sum up to one dollar,* and each of those were in turn to ask five friends, until, in less than two weeks, 45,000 people in the ghetto had been solicited and $25,000 had been raised.

Business is business and labor is labor and in Carl Stokes the twain seemed to have met. The AFL-CIO and the Teamsters' Union both promised "maximum efforts" on behalf of Stokes.

Labor, which had opposed Stokes so strongly in 1965, now forgot that he had opposed them on OBC and on apportionment, and suddenly remembered that as a legislator, he had worked in behalf of labor on minimum wage and on unemployment and workmen's compensation.

Only the nationality wards seemed to be holding out. Some of the Democratic councilmen running for re-election in cosmo wards had been reluctant to endorse the nominee. The relatively cold reception that Stokes had got on October 22 at the annual Night in Budapest party, and the enthusiastic cheers for Seth Taft by those normally Democratic party-goers, had made at least half of Cleveland's thirty-one Democratic councilmen wish they could simply disappear until after the election.

The Night in Budapest is a command performance for all Cleveland politicians. Once a year over two thousand Hungarians gather, in the words of the program notes: ". . . to honor the accomplishments of prominent Americans of Hungarian descent, and to refresh ourselves with the culture and cuisine of the land of the Magyars."

Though the evening is devoted to chicken paprikash and gypsy violins, and political speeches are not permitted, politicians are prominently on display, and no candidate for public office in Cleveland would dare not attend. Not even a bad case of food poisoning, which many of the guests had received from the cuisine of the land of the Magyars in 1964, had discouraged attendance in subsequent years.

Mayor Ralph Locher, a Rumanian who had spent many Nights in Budapest, was attending his last as mayor, and received the biggest cheer of the night as he took his seat. Seated strategically next to him, and receiving the second biggest ovation, was a non-Magyar, Seth Taft. Seated somewhat forlornly some distance away from these honored guests was another non-Magyar, Carl Stokes, who received only moderate applause when he was introduced.

It is frustrating for a man like Carl Stokes, who likes to talk to the people, to be in a gathering of two thousand and not be able to speak. He could only sit on the platform and be stared at by a hall full of Hungarians, who could at least see that he did not have two heads.

His friend, Zoltan Gombos, from *Szabadsag,* who acted as one of the toastmasters, did his best to make a public statement for Stokes without mentioning his name by saying that only in America could there be a Night in Budapest where people of all races, creeds, and nationalities could eat *toltott Kaposzta* and *sult kacsa* to the strains of a gypsy rhapsody, and go on together to build a greater Cleveland, where all people could find brotherhood as they and their fathers had.

The cosmo councilmen duly noted the meager applause that greeted Stokes, and squirmed uncomfortably when they were later asked by a reporter whether they were endorsing Stokes. None of them was willing to risk the future wrath of a Democratic city hall by endorsing Taft, but some were less than enthusiastic about Stokes.

"I am not endorsing," said one. "I didn't endorse in the primary."

Another said, "At the present time, I'm just concerned about myself."

But even the most reluctant Democratic councilmen were to go along when the Democratic executive committee made its official endorsement. Bert Porter had delayed calling the committee into session because of pressure from some of the nationality councilmen who feared that formal party endorsement of Stokes would require an open endorsement of him by each of them, thus jeopardizing their own re-election chances in their anti-Stokes wards. But when the White House said "Guess who's coming to dinner," and it was announced that Carl and Shirley Stokes would be the guests of Lyndon and Ladybird Johnson on October 26, a Democratic executive-committee meeting was hurriedly con-

vened for October 25 for the formal endorsement of
Carl Stokes. Though Stokes did not withdraw his demand that Porter resign, and though Porter did not
renounce the discredited Democratic news-letters at least
a superficial air of harmony prevailed at the meeting.
One of the pro-Stokes Negro councilmen praised Porter
generously from the floor, and the biggest ovation of
the evening came not for Stokes but for Porter when
city council president James Stanton moved that the
meeting "rise and give a standing vote of confidence
to our chairman." Stanton is the man who had given
Stokes a warm endorsement in Stanton's key west-side
ward, and the man with whom Stokes would have to
co-operate if he was to have a successful administration.
It was more important to keep Jim Stanton than to get
rid of Bert Porter

In spite of all the talk about outside influence and
Washington support, and the promise of Hubert Humphrey to come to Cleveland for Stokes if asked, the only
Washingtonian who actually made it to Cleveland for
the campaign was Seth's brother, Peter. Taft received
absolutely no help from Ohio's Republican governor.
Rhodes, first of all, had remembered Stokes's support in
the apportionment and bond-commission issues; more
to the point, however, he wasn't eager to see another
Taft come to political prominence in Ohio. One Taft
was in his way now, and he suspected that somewhere
in his political future lay a contest with Robert Taft,
Jr., probably for the Republican nomination to the
United States Senate in 1970.

Carl Stokes, meanwhile, had read the polls, showing what seemed to be the declining popularity of the national administration, and had advised Washington that he would be needing no outside speakers.

Finally the Cleveland *Plain Dealer,* which had given Stokes his first big impetus with its primary endorsement, completed the circle with a front-page statement that signaled the end of an era and the beginning of another:

> The *Plain Dealer* is endorsing Carl B. Stokes, Democrat, for mayor of Cleveland.
>
> We are endorsing him because—
>
> He has the determination, imagination, desire, and drive to find solutions to the many problems of this city.
>
> A Negro and a Democrat, he has appealed in his campaign to Clevelanders as a whole and has made clear that if elected, he would serve all his fellow Clevelanders fairly.
>
> A native Clevelander, Stokes shares, through a lifetime of personal experiences, the city's problems because he has grown up and lived with them at home and at work. He is a participant, not an outsider.
>
> Stokes has ample experience in working directly for the public, as a member of the Ohio House of Representatives, assistant police prosecutor, State Liquor Control agent, and probation officer. He has made public service his career.
>
> Voters in Cuyahoga County first showed their confidence in Stokes when he won election to the Ohio House from the county-at-large. Later, when the county was subdistricted, he won election from a district.
>
> He has been endorsed by Mayor Ralph Locher and by most of the rest of the city's leading Democrats.
>
> If Stokes becomes the first member of his race to be

elected mayor of a great city, he will bear a deep responsibility. He cannot afford to fail and he knows it. To govern well he cannot favor any special group and he knows it.

These are our major reasons for hoping that on November 7th the voters of this city will elect Carl B. Stokes mayor.

There are other reasons. We find Stokes a personable, articulate man who is well suited by temperament for a job that has become one of the most difficult and exacting in government. He has shown good judgment and balance.

Carl Stokes is opposed by the Republican nominee, Seth Taft, a well-meaning suburbanite who has headed several non-political civic organizations.

Taft, who moved in from Pepper Pike only to run for mayor, has served Cleveland in an advisory capacity but never as a public official.

The *Plain Dealer's* editors interviewed both candidates at length. Its reporters have followed the careers of both men and, in particular, their campaigns for office.

To us there is no comparison. Stokes is a skilled professional. Taft is merely a pleasant amateur.

The election is a little more than two weeks away. The *Plain Dealer* has waited until this late date to make its determination because we believe this election is the most important in Cleveland's history.

An era ended at city hall with the defeat of Mayor Locher. Great new horizons and a new civic life are possible for our marvelous city—with the right man as mayor.

Luckily, remarkably, we have the man capable to do the job. The *Plain Dealer* endorses Carl B. Stokes for mayor of Cleveland.

Now it was all over but the vote-counting. Carl Stokes was going to city hall and Seth Taft was going back to committee work.

In one sense, the Stokes administration was a success before it had even begun. There already seemed to be a rebirth of spirit in Cleveland. Carl Stokes had promised the city a boost for its sagging morale and he had already provided the boost. The country and the world were suddenly paying attention to Cleveland, and Cleveland was feeling good about it.

"I believe in Cleveland," Carl Stokes had told them. "That has been the theme of my campaign. . . ."

I believe the people of Cleveland have the intelligence to understand that our city is now mired in the mud of many problems.

Our basic problem is the widespread feeling of hopelessness and helplessness and general doubt that we can really solve these problems.

This depressing defeatism stems from the bewildered failures of the present administration.

These failures have caused untold misery, despair, and financial loss to every businessman and home owner. They have deprived our young people of opportunities to which they are entitled. They have hurt all of us—babies and senior citizens, bankers and busboys, housewives and industrialists.

I believe that the people of Cleveland recognize that our city needs a renaissance, a resurgence of faith in ourselves, a renewal of spirit and morale as well as a renewal of buildings and physical facilities.

I believe that the people of this city are aware that this renaissance must start with the election of a new mayor—a mayor who believes in Cleveland; a mayor who believes in the potential of people to rise to challenge; a mayor who has the capacity to enlist the best talents of our community in a crusade for a better Cleveland.

This is my program.

This is my promise.

I am beholden to no political boss or clique. I have no obligation or allegiance to any special interest group. I seek to serve all the people with dedication and devotion.

The election itself had already inspired "a renewal of spirit and morale," and nobody could say that that wasn't at least a good beginning. But the victory of Democrat Carl Stokes, which should have been a foregone conclusion in a heavily Democratic city, was to be decided by a margin of less than 1 per cent of the total votes. Racial fear had done its job.

21. THE MAYOR

ON NOVEMBER 7 the eyes of the country were focused on Cleveland, Ohio, with sidelong glances at Boston, Massachusetts, where Louise Day Hicks was expected to demonstrate the power of white backlash, and at Gary, Indiana, where Negro mayoral candidate Richard Hatcher, still fighting the Gary Democratic party, found his campaign enmeshed in state and federal courts with the Indiana national guard standing by to police either the election or its aftermath.

What was less well known was that the Ohio national guard had also been alerted and was standing by in an armory in Shaker Heights just outside the Cleveland city limits, at the request either of Mayor Locher or of Governor Rhodes, under the new power granted to him by Carl Stokes's anti-riot bill. Fortunately, the troops were not needed—but there were many in Cleveland on election night who expected that they would be.

Until after midnight it looked as if Stokes, in spite of the almost unanimous support of most of the institutions that usually determine the outcome of elections in Cleveland, would lose the election to Seth Taft. Both the *Press* and the *Plain Dealer* had repeated their endorsements on the day before the election. The AFL-CIO and the Teamsters had conducted mail and telephone campaigns for him. A large part of the business establishment had supported him. And the Democratic party had made him their official candidate (though party headquarters, which had bombarded party members with almost daily mailings in the primary for Locher and against Stokes, distributed virtually no pro-Stokes literature during the entire election campaign).

But despite all this support, which would have given the election to almost any white Democrat by at least 75,000 votes, by 9:00 P.M. press, radio, and TV were confidently forecasting a Taft victory, and an hour later even the Stokes vote-tabulating machinery, which had been so uncannily accurate in the primary, indicated that Taft would win by between 5,000 and 9,000 votes. But, to the vast relief of the Stokes workers, their tabulations and projections proved to be wrong. At 3:00 A.M. on November 8, when the last precinct had finally been recorded by the Board of Elections, Stokes was the winner and new mayor of Cleveland by 2,501 votes.

Stokes had increased his white-vote total of 18,000 in the primary to approximately 35,000 in the general election, and had taken over 20 per cent of the white vote. He had even increased his vote in the cosmo wards to close to 20 per cent—the wards where two years before he had received less than 2 per cent of the votes—and his Negro vote to 96 per cent. There were five Negro precincts none of which gave Taft a single vote but each of which gave Stokes approximately three hundred.

Earlier in the evening, Stokes had been prepared to appear on television with a concession speech and to begin what surely would have been a long delicate program of trying to keep the bitterness and frustration of the Negro community from exploding into rage. Happily, he never had to make the speech. Instead, he was able to say:

> What should be realized here is that this was not a Carl Stokes victory. This was a victory for a program, for a dream of what our city can do, can become.
>
> I'm calling for support of all the residents of this city. Hungarian, Lithuanian, Italian, Irish, Negro—all who have helped to build Cleveland into a place where a Carl Stokes could run for mayor and win . . . I call upon all of them now—now that we have resolved this question in the

great American tradition—I ask them to come with me
and build a great and renowned city.

I can say to you that never before have I ever known
the full meaning of the words "God Bless America."

Seth Taft, who probably had never expected to come
so close, seemed almost relieved as he made his concession speech:

> I wish that we will all think of the things that can be
> done in the future to make ours a great city. More than
> ever, we must now work together to solve the problems of
> human relations and I mean work wholeheartedly under
> the leadership of Mayor Stokes.

One week later Taft indicated that he was not quite
ready to "work wholeheartedly under the leadership of
Mayor Stokes" when, under pressure from the Republican party, he called for a recount of the vote. The recount was duly held, at a cost of $9,030 to Taft, but
changed only a handful of votes. Stokes had paid a like
amount for a recount in 1965 which likewise changed
only a few votes. Including his 1960 recount in the
legislature race, Stokes had thus been involved in three
recounts in seven years. He has had to fight hard for
every step forward in his political career, but though
he no longer uses his fists, he still enjoys a good fight.

With only three hours' sleep on November 8, and one
week before he was to be sworn in as mayor of Cleveland, Carl Stokes was already embarked on his crusade
when he addressed a Future of Cleveland luncheon as
mayor-elect:

We're going to show all the world that the people of a great American city can unite to solve the problems which, left unsolved, threaten to dissolve our urban civilization.

We won't look back on the divisive political campaign which ended in the early hours today. There are no recriminations, no retaliations, no grudges. The past is over, except as a base on which to build for the future.

There is no doubt in my mind that in the next few years we will show the world that the people of an American city can rise to meet the challenge.

Cleveland and other cities need and must have a spiritual and physical renaissance. By uniting, all Clevelanders can help the American dream—the Cleveland dream—come true!

The American dream was indeed looking a little better on November 8, 1967, in Boston, where Kevin White had triumphed over white backlash, in Gary, where the national guard had not been needed after Richard Hatcher's victory, and in Cleveland, where Carl Stokes was receiving congratulations from around the world.

There are those who say that the election of a Negro mayor in Cleveland, Ohio, in 1967 has only numerical significance; that with the flight of whites to the suburbs, it was inevitable that some northern metropolis in this decade would have a Negro mayor. It was just an accident, they say, that it happened first in Cleveland.

But if it was an accident, it was an accident that Carl Stokes made happen. There are other northern cities with a larger percentage of Negro residents, and if it was purely a question of numbers, it would have happened in one of those cities first. Neither was it just a simple case of the right man being in the right place at the right time. To a very large extent, Carl Stokes had helped to shape the forces that made 1967 the right year and Cleveland, Ohio, the right place. For ten years he had single-mindedly pursued the goal he had set for himself. He had seen the gap widening between the white community and the black community, and he knew that it had to be narrowed before the city's problems could be solved. And all that time he had straddled that chasm with one foot in the white world and one foot in the black, staunchly resisting all efforts from either side to push him into the abyss. The gap did indeed seem to be narrowing. That is the real significance and the real hope of the election of Carl Stokes. His entire political career has been motivated by his conviction that the races can live in harmony in this country. He knows that unless he is right about this, all the housecleaning and housekeeping that city government can devise will be futile.

Carl Stokes had been subjected to the most extreme pressures that any candidate for public office has had to endure, but he entered office with no commitments save the one with which he started his political career— his commitment to the belief that our political system can solve its urban crisis with the same application of ingenuity, talent, and determination that created the country and the cities; the universities and the space ships; the industrial might and the museums; the material wealth and the art. He would recruit that kind of talent and apply it to city government. There are those who maintain that the cities are beyond repair and that the traditional concepts of local government are obsolete and inadequate for the massive job required. Carl Stokes thinks otherwise. One of the contributing factors to urban decay has been eradicated with the reapportionment of state legislative bodies; now that urban representatives have the controlling voice in the state legislature, Stokes expects the state to be more responsive to urban needs. The knowledge that he gained as a member of the Ohio legislature and the friends that he made there will be immediately put to use in that direction. That, and his friendship with Governor Rhodes, should provide Cleveland with the best relationship it has ever enjoyed with state government, and will enable the Stokes administration to make the fullest possible use of whatever assistance might be available on a state level.

And then, of course, he is relying on his close ties with the national administration to enable him to get for Cleveland the maximum amount of federal assistance. It will not be easy: the giant shadow cast by the Vietnam war now extends to the whole country. It is no longer possible for a public figure at any government level to avoid questions on Vietnam. Carl Stokes, of course, had also been approached on this issue, but confined himself to saying only that he supported the position of the administration. (He is too dependent on federal aid to Cleveland to risk alienating a vindictive President.) In the closing days of the campaign, he had been asked at a university meeting whether he approved of the diversion of funds for the war on poverty into defense funds for the war in Vietnam. He had answered that of course he disapproved, and criticized Congress for its attempt to cut poverty funds. To which Seth Taft immediately responded with the charge that Stokes had reversed his position on Vietnam. No such thing, Stokes replied: he still supported the administration, but he thought the nation could and must, for as long as the war continued, provide butter as well as guns.

This country may possess the resources to provide both guns and butter, but it does not appear to have the inclination to do so. Two of the programs upon which Carl Stokes was relying—the Model Cities Act and the Rent Supplement Bill—have encountered strong resistance in Congress, and the entire poverty program is in jeopardy and will probably remain so until there is peace in Vietnam.

When Martin Luther King began opposing the war on the ground that, among other things, it would divert the country's attention and resources from the attack on the crisis of the cities, he was, as perhaps befits a prophet, almost a lone voice among the moderate civil-rights leaders who claimed that the one issue should have nothing to do with the other. But of course it does, and in time Carl Stokes may be forced, as Congress apparently believes it has been, to express a choice between guns and butter.

And there will be pressures of other kinds from all directions. He will be watched carefully by the black nationalists, because to the extent that he succeeds in his goal of unifying the city, they will fail in their aim to tear it apart. There will be many suspicious whites who will claim favoritism to Negroes on the slightest pretext. There will be disappointed Clevelanders who will complain that what thirty years of neglect has done to Cleveland, Carl Stokes has been unable to correct. Because he is the first, there will be a tendency to add the dimension of color to everything he does as mayor. He must be mayor to all, but he will also be, whether he likes it or not, a representative of his race. Both races will impose that role upon him, as they will his symbolic role as a demonstration of democracy.

One of his first cabinet appointments was influenced, in large part, by a kind of pressure no white mayor has ever had to face. Under the Cleveland city charter the law director, appointed by the mayor, becomes acting mayor in the mayor's absence and automatically succeeds him in the event of his death or disability. The law directorship is, therefore, the most important position in the cabinet. After first publicly announcing that he would not appoint a Negro as law director, he changed his mind. It was generally assumed that he had responded to pressure from the Negro community, but, in fact, his appointment of a Negro law director was a form of life insurance for himself. His election had intensified the threats of violence on his person and his life, and he reasoned that an insane racist with murder on his mind might be deterred by the realization that the removal of Carl Stokes would result only in another Negro mayor.

The man appointed, Judge Paul White, is highly qualified for the position, and his appointment was praised by the newspapers. However, the *Cleveland Tribunal,* a more or less underground paper that seems to be a mish-mash of black-nationalist and new-left ideas, and that characteristically complained about the mayor's appointments, had this sour note to sound in its first issue following the election:

> Talking about jobs: Stokes offered M. Morris Jackson the job of service director and Jackson turned it down. Black men are tired of being in charge of garbage collection.

The article in which this complaint was registered was written by Lewis Robinson, of J.F.K. House, erstwhile Stokes supporter. But, aside from the expected grumbles of a few other black nationalists, who must attack in order to exist, Cleveland so far is more than pleased with Mayor Stokes, and he will probably enjoy a longer honeymoon than most new executives. For the time being, at least, Negro youth in Cleveland has a new idol, and Stokes is determined not to lose them back to the nationalists. Less than a month after the election he made an unpublicized appearance at Glenville High School, where, to thundering ovations, he made an inspirational speech to the all-Negro student body. He told them that by the time they were forty, as he was, there would be no limit to their horizons and that education was the magic key that would open new doors for them. He warned them against false prophets and doom criers in the streets. He conceded that there was still a long way to go but urged them to recognize that progress was being made in the only way it could be made—within the democratic process. He closed by telling the story of the old Negro lady during reconstruction in Mississippi who had been a slave all her life and now saw all about her Negroes who were not only free but who were also legislators, lawyers, judges, and congressmen, and said:

> We ain't what we wanna be
> We ain't what we oughta be
> We ain't what we gonna be
> But, Great God, we sure ain't what we was.

It was an appropriate story and the students loved it, but there is surely bitter irony in the fact that stories like it must have been told with the same optimism one hundred years ago. And most of the students were probably too young to remember the hopes that were inspired by the 1954 segregation decisions and that were still unrealized, or the promise that was offered in the civil-rights acts of the last decade and that was still unfulfilled. There have been too many false starts; and Carl Stokes and others like him may represent the last best hope for the Glenville students and for the rest of us.

It is still too early for an accurate appraisal of the Stokes administration, but he has taken hold with a firm and confident grasp, and Cleveland at last has the feeling that it is being led. The problems of the city are vast indeed, but beyond repair? Carl Stokes doesn't think so. He is not yet ready to concede that we have forgotten the art of governing ourselves.

One thing is clear—his administration might fail, but not for ignorance of the ills that plague Cleveland. Stokes had studied city hall for ten years. He would know how to deal with city council because he himself had been a legislator. He would understand the problems of police administration because he himself had been a law-enforcement officer. And when he talked about slums, it would be more than mere rhetoric—he had lived on that side of the tracks.

> We know that Cleveland, along with every major city in America, is now in a period of crisis. Physically, the heart of our city is in a condition of decay that calls for major surgery and rebuilding. Commensurate with and resulting from the physical decay, the human conditions have become intolerable and inexcusable.

> How, for example, can anyone justify the human misery, the hovels that house thousands of families, the degradation of life in reeking slums with leaky plumbing and sometimes no plumbing, the horrible atmosphere in which young children must live? How can anyone justify these conditions in what has always been the land of opportunity?

Seth Taft had accurately summed up those conditions by saying: "Cleveland is in the midst of a crisis of human relations." But though he had recognized the problem and had defined it, it no longer seemed possible for a

Taft to solve it. The world had changed too much for that. The Stokes era of urban politics was about to begin.

The election of Carl Stokes may help to restrain the violence and rioting that has erupted out of resentment of a century of second-class citizenship for Negroes in our society. But there will continue to be incidents of violence so long as the underlying conditions that feed it go uncorrected. That is why Carl Stokes says: "The biggest challenge we face today is the urgent need to eradicate these conditions, to perform major surgery on our city . . ." A task that will take more than city hall alone, one that may well require the establishment of a new order of social and economic priorities on a national scale.

The job will take many years and Carl Stokes will be gone from city hall before it is finished. As his political career has progressed, he has attracted increasingly large numbers of white supporters. With the greater exposure that his new office will provide, and his image as a nationally known political figure, Ohio voters outside of Cleveland will feel the impact of the Stokes personality. Others, not Ohioans, have already felt it. Murray Kempton, of the *New York Post,* who heard Stokes address a businessmen's luncheon in New York, reported:

> When Mayor Stokes arose, it became impossible not to believe that Cleveland must be the most bigoted town on earth if sixty per cent of its white citizens did not automatically vote for him. His style is the easiest sort of charm, with just the proper flavor of the unobtrusively earnest; he is also shrewd enough to know that his success

as a mayor depends on no ultimate mystery of government except the art of getting business to trust you. His allusions to his own identity could not have been more delicate; his fervor was reserved for his welcome to industrial capital.

And, following the President's 1968 State of the Union message, Stokes more than held his own on a nationwide television program with such heavy hitters as economists Walter Heller and Milton Friedman, publisher Bill Moyers, urbanologist Pat Moynihan, and those aging *enfants terrible,* William F. Buckley, Jr., and Arthur Schlesinger, Jr. (the "Jr." appendages seemed appropriate, since these two spent most of the evening attacking each other on the level of "my dad can lick your dad"). Stokes was forced to admit, on this program, that the President's message promised more guns and less butter.

Cleveland is Ohio's largest city, but it is also its most provincial, and it is likely that Carl Stokes will be more readily accepted as a candidate in other, more sophisticated urban areas. His popularity in polls has always been highest among the younger and the more educated voters, and it is quite possible that in a few years he could be a serious candidate for governor or for the United States Senate.

Senator Robert Kennedy, when he was still Attorney General, once made a speech on civil rights in which he suggested that it was conceivable that there would be a Negro President by 1980. Robert Kennedy, unhappily and tragically, is gone, but Carl Stokes may yet fulfill his prophecy.

Afterword

B Y THE time this book appears, Carl B. Stokes will have completed almost half his first term as mayor of Cleveland. A year is hardly time enough to assess a city's problems, let alone cure them. But a start has been made.

Within a few months after his election, Stokes succeeded in having Cleveland's frozen urban-renewal funds restored by the Department of Housing and Urban Development. The funds are certain to be administered more wisely than in the past because for the first time Cleveland has a qualified, experienced renewal expert to run its Community Development Department. In order to lure Richard Green from Boston, where he had done impressive work under Ed Logue, Stokes first had to convince a reluctant city council to authorize a salary of $30,000 a year—$5,000 more than his honor himself makes. There is little chance that a city council which thought it was being profligate in raising salaries to a barely respectable level in order to attract competent experts to city government will provide the funds needed to bring Cleveland all the way into the twentieth century. Stokes's proposal of an increase in city income taxes so that the general salary level of city employees might be raised has consistently been met with resistance. An unfortunate error in timing, if not in judgment, may have seriously compromised his chances of getting the tax increase.

Stokes, with his finely tailored suits, his expensive cigars, his careful grooming, and his graceful personal style, is very conscious of his image. Early in his administration he decided to take a small step in the direction of upgrading Cleveland's image. He thought that Cleveland should symbolically leave the horse and buggy age by acquiring an expensive limousine to convey VIPs on Cleveland visits. The $11,000 requisition was scarcely noticed as it began its circuit through the bureaucratic maze, but one month later it hit the headlines simultaneously with Stokes's announcement that a review of the city's finances indicated a need for a tax increase. Cleveland, always eager for any excuse to avoid facing reality, was happy to seize upon the $11,000 automobile, and Stokes was forced to cancel the limousine purchase. Even with a substantial tax increase, however, Cleveland couldn't hope to meet its needs with the revenue from local sources alone. Massive federal assistance will be needed, and it is becoming increasingly clear to Carl Stokes that the Vietnam war precludes that assistance. Though he has privately confided to friends his opposition to the war, his public stance is still one of support of the national administration. He is, in a sense, a hostage to LBJ's war policies. In this area, his personal ambitions have come into violent conflict with his personal convictions. Were he to openly express his opposition to the war, he would run the risk, not only of alienating Washington but also of losing his favored position as one of the Democratic party's brightest new stars. He has already made several national appearances for the party, and there is a movement afoot to have him make one of the nominating speeches at the Democratic national convention. No doubt Carl Stokes wishes that Vietnam would simply go away—like the rest of the country does.

Stokes has made significant progress, however, in those areas not requiring the expenditure of additional funds. To an extent not thought possible a year ago, he has tempered the hostility between Cleveland's police and the black community. One of his first acts as mayor was to order the removal of the white riot helmets that Cleveland's police had worn at all times since the Hough riots of 1966. Cleveland no longer seems like a city under siege. Fighting a deeply entrenched police bureaucracy, he has reorganized the department to put more officers on the streets in high-crime areas. There has already been some evidence of a decrease in crime, but, more important, Stokes's insistence that all citizens be treated by the police with courtesy and dignity has created a more promising atmosphere for citizen-police relationships.

On the labor front, Stokes has, as he promised in his campaign, helped to settle a year-long strike against one of the city's largest hospitals by its non-professional employees, most of them Negro. Their battle for higher wages had occasionally erupted into violence and had further exacerbated racial tensions in Cleveland. Stokes was thought foolish by some of his advisers for promising to intervene in what appeared to be a hopelessly deadlocked situation. And when his initial efforts failed, he was criticized by some (including the *New York Times Magazine* in a premature hundred-day report on the Stokes administration) for having considered intervening in the first place. But Stokes persisted, and it was largely through his efforts that the strike was settled. He is not afraid to fail, which is one of the reasons why he probably won't.

The business community, which had lost confidence in the previous administration, seems happy with Stokes, and several prominent members of the business establishment have taken jobs with the administration. Stokes has succeeded in having council enact Port Authority legislation, something Cleveland had wanted but had been unable to get for many years. He has created a bold new program called Cleveland Now, which, with a combination of private money and federal funds, may set a pattern for urban rehabilitation throughout the country. He has involved private citizens in the project to an extent never before seen in Cleveland.

It has not, of course, been smooth sailing all the way. He has made some mistakes and he has had some bad breaks. Geraldine Williams is a case in point. Miss Williams, a prominent figure in the Negro community, had been one of Stokes's most effective campaigners in both 1965 and 1967. After the election she was made an administrative assistant to the mayor and served as a valuable link to the Negro community—especially to its more militant elements. Two months after he took office, Stokes, exhausted from the campaign and eighteen-hour days as a new mayor trying to discover what had been happening at city hall for the past thirty years, left town for a short vacation. While he was gone, the *Cleveland Press,* in headlines larger than it had devoted to many serious problems of the city, charged that Geraldine Williams had been a partner in a saloon in the Negro ghetto and had operated the saloon as a so-called cheat spot, illegally serving liquor after hours and on Sundays. How this charge, even if true, could have affected her competence as a city employee did not concern the *Press,* and if Stokes had been in town, it is likely that he could have finessed the whole trivial matter. But he was not in town, and when Miss Williams and nervous assistants at city hall began making conflicting statements to persistent reporters, the incident was blown out of all proportion, resulting in Miss Williams' being fired.

That this ever became an issue is perhaps a measure of the job Carl Stokes faces in his desire to promote understanding between blacks and whites. The white community, whose puritan soul seems to require prohibition in at least some degree, appears to be overly obsessed with the drinking habits of the black community. It was a cheat spot that led to the first "scandal" of the Stokes administration and it was a raid on a ghetto cheat spot in Detroit (there called a blind pig) that triggered the Detroit riots of 1967.

Stokes was forced to discharge another assistant, this one a prominent white lawyer, who was shot in the shoulder by a jealous husband who had caught the lawyer, if not in *flagrante delicto,* then at least in suspicious circumstances, in the home of the husband's estranged wife. It later turned out that this same assistant had failed to file federal income-tax returns for several years, so if sex had not brought him down, taxes would have. It is interesting, if melancholy, to note that the Cleveland newspapers devoted much more space to the question of whether or not a Negro woman might have been serving liquor illegally than they did to the unquestioned fact that a prominent and successful white lawyer had failed to file tax returns.

Stokes's other appointments, made after the pressure of hastily organizing a new administration had let up have been more successful and of generally high caliber, despite the low salary scale.

All things considered, the Stokes administration is off to a good start. Even the *Cleveland Press* had to admit in its spring report: "In sum, it shows beginnings to have been made in several important sectors." At the same time, the *New York Times* carried the headline: "Negro Mayor's Program in Cleveland Shows Gains."

The Cleveland *Plain Dealer* reported in March, following a Stokes Washington visit:

> On balance, as they like to say in this town, Mayor Carl B. Stokes made a very good impression on the federal bureaucracy during his visit here this past week. Stokes also came over solidly with the Johnson administration. His impact was not so much due to his magnetic personality and flashing appeal to the crowd—it's not easy to impress a fellow politician alone at a desk—but much more because of Stokes's earnestness and candor.

On the personal level, Stokes has been an unqualified success. He has made several impressive national television appearances, and will undoubtedly play a vital role in the national Democratic campaign in 1968, no matter who the candidate. Supporters of each possible candidate have eagerly solicited his support. That support, however, is already pledged to Vice President Humphrey, and the Stokes stock has risen several more points. His message is the same one with which he started his career. A massive attack must be made on the economic problems of black America, and Negroes must be convinced that political activity can help them become full partners in American society. No one has offered a better prescription for America's racial ills. Stokes believes that separatism is defeatism, and hopes that his own practical demonstration of black political power can give enough hope to enough Negroes to save the country from the extremists, black and white, right and left. It is clear that he has restored hope to Cleveland's Negroes, who seem willing to tolerate intolerable conditions for a little while longer.

"I don't expect any racial upheavals this summer," one of the local Negro leaders has said. "Simply because of the protective attitude of the great majority of Negroes here toward the Mayor."

Even the more militant elements of the black community seem satisfied: "He's doing an excellent job," said the local CORE leader. "We recognize the obstacles he is facing in trying to serve all the people."

That "protective attitude" stood Stokes in good stead when, in perhaps his finest hour to date, he was able to secure the cooperation of militant Negro leaders in keeping Cleveland peaceful while most other large urban areas reacted violently to the assassination of Martin Luther King.

Stokes's election has given Negroes a new awareness of the potential of black political power, and Negro political organization and activity has been spurred throughout the country. Clearly, Ohio politics will never be the same. The Stokes name has won Brother Lou an unexpected victory in a congressional primary, and Negro resentment of Frank Lausche's failure to support Carl Stokes was one of the most important factors in John Gilligan's victory over Lausche.

Meanwhile, Stokes has been busy spreading his gospel. At a Democratic fund-raising dinner in Los Angeles he said:

> If we fail today to take strong and broad action on all fronts, those who would be satisfied with the status quo, or even worse, those reactionaries who would move backwards, will use our failures to justify their own programs of anti-progress. The voices of our critics will be more rancorous. Our failures will be magnified. . . . Then we will witness the worst of all crises; for our cities will be undone.

One of the most rancorous voices that concerns Stokes belongs to another former Golden Gloves boxer who turned to politics and has come to national prominence largely on the question of race. Ex-Governor George Wallace of Alabama, sometimes a Democrat but more often a demagogue, unlike Democrat Carl Stokes with his message of hope, preaches fear and force. Wallace has staked his future on his conviction that this country's racial problem cannot be solved. There are black extremists who have staked their futures on the same proposition. George Wallace wants to get to the White House, and he believes racial fear will take him there. If the black extremists and the black and white prophets of doom are right, he may make it someday. Carl Stokes would no doubt like to make it to the White House also, but he is enough of a political realist to realize that his chances are slim. But if Carl Stokes is right in his conviction that the American political system is strong enough, imaginative enough, determined enough to solve its racial problem, then at least we will be spared George Wallace.

Mr. Wallace, meet Mr. Stokes.

Index

A Note on the Author

Kenneth G. Weinberg was born in Akron, Ohio, and studied at Miami University (Ohio) and the Harvard Law School. As a practicing attorney he has been active politically, has served as counsel to the federal government and the State of Ohio, and was the lawyer in the Supreme Court case which required reapportionment of the Ohio legislature. Mr. Weinberg is a partner in the firm of Gottfried, Ginsberg, Guren and Merritt in Cleveland, where he lives with his wife, Helen, and their three children.